That eros knows nothing

Of the word better

Our only hope

All's fair

In love and war

Our every demise

Katy Bohinc

Dear Alain

TENDER BUTTONS PRESS

New York City

2014

Tender Buttons Press
New York, New York
www.TenderButtonsPress.com

Cover Design Cassandra Gillig
Interior Design Wayne Smith
Text set in Cambria Math

Interior Artworks
Tender Buttons Drawing by Joe Brainard, printed with permission
Natal Chart Wheel by Cafe Astrology, CafeAstrology.com
Drawings by Katy Bohinc
Malcolm X Park image from the National Park Service www.nps.gov

Cataloguing-in-publication data available
From the Library of Congress
ISBN 978-0-927920-11-7

Printed by BookMobile

Selections of this work have appeared in *Where Eagles Dare*, *Armed Cell*, *Open Letters Monthly*, *Elderly*, *Elective Affinities*, and *& Now Awards 3: The Best Innovative Writing*. Much thanks to *Summer BF Press* who also published a small selection of the letters as an objet d'art.

For Christina

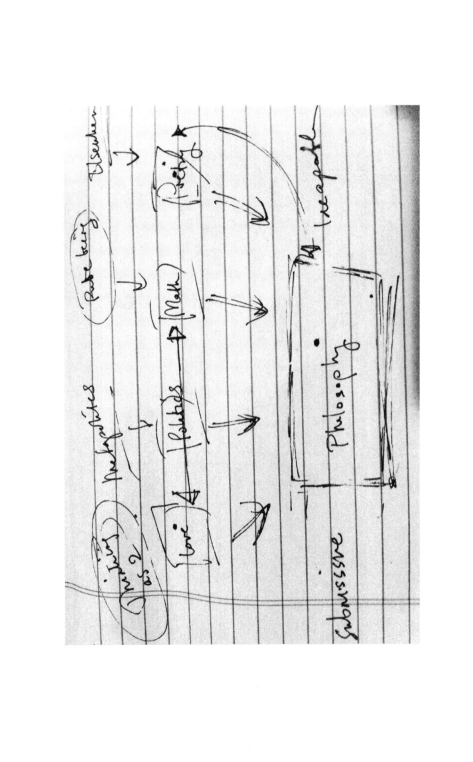

Let us add that contemporary philosophy addresses itself at all times to women. It might even be suspected that it is, as discourse, partly a strategy of seduction.

Alain Badiou, "What is Love?"

You dare to study philosophy baby I'll tell you
About fucking Aristotle I never planned to fall
In love with you who often happen by where I am
Let me hide you amidst the sublime responsibility you are

Bernadette Mayer, SONNET

Let us agree to call k(x) the Katy function,
and a(x) the Alain function

$$\sum_{0}^{\infty} k_n + \alpha_n$$

This the poem a summation of two functions

Terms: As Defined by the philosopher Alain Badiou

Philosophy: System describing how truth is produced
Love: Thinking as Two
Politics: Revolution
Poetry: Elsewhere
Math: Pure Being
The Event: That which produces truth
The Event of Love: The declaration of "I love you"
Truth: Singularity
Evil: Naming the Unnamable

Terms: As defined by the poet katy bohinc

Philosophy: My bitch
Love: The source & the glue
Politics: Problematic unless approaching infinity
Poetry: Everything
Math: The origin
The Event: The Kernal
The Event of Love: At first sight
Truth: The lowest and highest tones
Evil: Pain

Conditions of Alain Badiou imposed on this work:

1. *The concepts of Alain Badiou's philosophy shall condition this text.*

2. *The poet shall critique the philosopher, as poetry is a condition on philosophy.*

3. *The poet and the philosopher shall begin to think as two, as determined by their love.*

4. *The obvious conflict proceeding shall be the process of this work.*

5. *The event shall be the determination of said conflict.*

6. *The poet will discuss concepts of Poetry – those of Alain and those of her own.*

7. *The poet will discuss infinity - those ideas of Alain and those of her own.*

8. *The poet will condition her lover the philosopher with mathematics, politics, ideas of language, ideas of evil, ideas of naming, ideas of the void, ideas of historicity, ideas of the West, ideas of astrology, ideas of play, ideas of cliché, singularity, oneness, appearance, Marxism, multiplicity, etc.*

9. *The concept of Condition will be complicated, as will most the philosopher's ideas, as the poet is prone to insult the philosopher, like any good (?) lover. It is not so much a point as an effect that here Alain is a condition. Or, peut-être, non?*

10. *The relations and narrative shall generally be ambiguous so as to grant the reader multiple possible interpretations. Construct your truth.*

11. *Let us add, that contemporary poetry addresses itself at all times to "men". It might even be said it is a matter of seduction.*

"Poem, Matheme, Politics and Love at once condition and insult philosophy. Condition and insult: that's the way it is." – A.B.

$$k_0 + \alpha_0$$

"It is fixed only by a nomination, and this nomination is a declaration, the declaration of love." – A.B.

Dear Alain,

There, got it, round two. multiplicity. said Badiou. you mother fucker stole my brain. except, you're wrong. still working in euclid's plane. enlightenment is the real projective. where parallel lines meet at the horizon and a line is a circle. it's true that the abrahamic religions have a problem with historicity and crusades. somebody's always got to be right before and in order to get to God. buddha knows the line is really a circle at the horizon anyway, where we all should strive to dwell. the point, it's a line. the line, it's a circle. the circle, it's a flower. that point derrida collapsed in the derivatives market? don't worry about it. we'll fix it when we wake up. cat life number 27, ladybug reincarnate.

Dear Alain,

The isolated hysteria of city dwelling. Universal truth? You're crying alone. You're crying alone. And there's something wrong here. Don't make sense to go bowling alone, no bone cold enough for a life like that. We got to get some meatloaf and gravy on this table, live humans creaking in the chairs, laughter cracking up the atmosphere, bring your tears here, bring em drippin down your nose long and heavy we'll cook those boys to the corners with friendship sweet and mighty. Laughter tears are good for wrinkles.

Wink, K

Dear Alain,

I think when you talk about Multiplicity, Alain, really didn't a guy named Hardt write that ten years back? I guess he was riffing on you but it led him to Classicism. Chaos is the original sin we've been running from all our architectural lives. Why are we spending our energy re-discovering this? Why does this constitute a form we want to represent? Is it that we never knew how bad it could be until Hitler? Maybe we didn't know how much pain dissolves brick. I see this as the real problem.

Dear Alain

I want to meet you very badly and write you love poems. I want to
know where you put love in your schema; if you believe in it. Did
you ever read Zamyatin's "We"? It's what Orwell based 1984 on.
He got kicked out of Russia before it was Bolshevik. But Zamyatin
foretold a world where everything was algebra and the only thing
to wake up the creativity, the poetry pole you juxtapose like math,
the Dionysius to your linear Apollo, well let's just say Dionysius
didn't dance without Venus. Do you think Venus exists? You must
believe in the ***, the undefined, the ***, the poetry that beds the
data when it's young and vomiting on the floor, before it grows
into a tall and strong polynomial chain. You said you did. Back
to that Hardt guy, he ended up talking about love too and I think
that's where his career ended. Nobody wants to listen to the
mushy stuff. But I gotta tell you, my friend Chad B said it best:
"I don't care if you're the tiny-ist, whiney-ist, most pampered
cheerleader or the hood-est, hard-est most jock football player,
everybody got somebody put em fetal in the kitchen make em bat
shit crazy." Is this the constant in the incompleteness theorem?
Desire? I hate that word. What about capital L Love? Should I just
ask somebody to write me a prescription and forget about it?

Dear Alain,

I recognize that I am being sassy, immature and superficial. However, it seems that love poems are out of style. (I'm still terribly upset about that). I honestly would like to know what you think Monsieur Badiou. Also, I read your essay on Mallarme. It seems clear that you are a philosopher and not a poet. I am deeply grateful you write of poetry at all. Your analysis, its geometry is well mapped. Perhaps I wish to go a bit further outside the language of being/event and say more simply, poetry is the undefinable. I think it should be off the map entirely! I think you would agree if you envision it in terms of an x-y coordinate axis, but I must point out my logical inconsistency -- where is poetry if it does not exist on the plane? A strong argument for a third dimension. Emotions, maybe. The soul. Magic. Stuff like that. Or, back to classical Euclid, it would be very poetic to say poetry is the origin. Exactly (0,0). I like that. Poetry at the Origin. Capital O. How orgasmic!

Dear Alain,

Oh Monsieur Badiou! How lovely to argue with you! Thank you dearly and I look forward to fucking you again soon. Really, I am a big prude. I rarely fuck in public. Please take this as a token of my deepest admiration and affection. Next time, in French! And in French fashion, now that I have told you all the things I don't like about you, we can be friends. I shall try to proceed in pure devotion to all your most finest accomplishments.

Yours, Katy

Dear Alain,

Forgive me. Burn these letters. I forgot to write "par avion".
Perhaps they will not arrive. I dearly hope so. Burn them.
Please. I will be a better student. I will be more serious.
Do not forsake me.

Yours,
Katy

Dear Alain,

I thought all day of what I would write you. Now I can merely see my fingers typing at the keys. Everything escapes me. My mind thinks of so many intimate things to tell you: what I think of your work, how I feel, the images and the selflessness. When I think of writing for the entire of existence, of humanity, I am in church with a vow to serious straight eyes, concentration, a heavy heart and good posture. It terrifies me and makes me cry. How do you do it?

Love, Katy

Dear Alain,

If it is the continuation of the canon that allows you to make incremental progress in the works of philosophy, then how do you not wonder if the canon has made a mistake? I do not mean your discussions with Derrida or Heidegger. I wonder if we are not profoundly mistaken. You discuss life as if set theory could approach it. I admire the "limitless-ness" of your approach, in that calculus has no limit in having a limit. But politics! I fear we are so near the end that philosophy is merely a performative architecture, rather than a salvation we need. I mean, possibly Red Scare...but isn't global warming real? Do I confuse truth with answers, and a way to think with a way to live? Perhaps I should compartmentalize you in the "philosophy" division, and not ask you questions of basic moral existence.

Is too much to ask? But you said, you do not like specialization. Should I look in the "self-help" section? I cannot help but consider you from the view of the ignorant. For I sense I am completely blind. I would say we are completely blind, but to speak beyond any other than myself seems a treason. Then again I wish with all my ego to say "everything is X". Is it the history or the graph that makes it easier for you? These words, Being and Event. They seem a trick of logic which remove responsibility. Everything is timeless before death, unless you consider pregnancy.

Truly, Katy

Dear Alain,

I thought being with you, openly, brazenly, could be so many things. I thought you would understand me, I thought I could be naked before you. There would be profundity and confession. You see as poets we dance. I could say to you "now against the wall" but i've tried this before and it doesn't work as well as you'd think. So we play a game, an artifice, a style a form to get to that ee cummings moment in the poem. I wondered if I could be myself for you, and be quite serious and earnest with all my passion because you are serious and earnest. But perhaps we amount to giggles because can't bare our wretched infinite. Oh dear, I am torn between my artifice and intimacy. Be patient with me. I wish at once to ease your tired ears but also to put light to these deepest thoughts we never say aloud. Perhaps the things that matter most.

When tomorrow becomes yesterday and tomorrow becomes eternity when the soul with the soul goes way beyond

Yours, Katy

Dear Alain,

Forgive me. It was the whiskey last night. I speak too quickly and with too little thought. I will be more serious. As clear as a winter landscape for you.

A ce soir,
Kati

Alain,

Please, write soon. Your silences always depress me. Or perhaps it is that thinking like a philosopher may be suicidal. You metal jungle gym!

As always, you are the eternal object of my being and I hope to pass an event with you soon.

Yours, Katy

Affair #1

Dear Julian,

Meet me in rat alley by the old mattress. The Four Seasons is for criminals.

In code,
Katya

Dear Alain,

Philosophers and poets, we're both trying to reach God, you the form, we the content. You the throne, we the light.

Thoughtfully, Katy

Dear Alain,

I'm sick from being serious. I'm sick of this fucking shit. Speaking
to you on your terms in your vocabulary requires a tired
precision I loathe. I like monkeys and raspberries and autumn
squash cooked for one hour at 350 degrees Fahrenheit with a
glaze of two tablespoons butter, agave nectar and dijon mustard.
Lightly speckled with pepper. I don't mean the cooking channel.
I mean John Coltrane for Lovers on repeat because it's Sunday,
the holiday of the sun regime from 300 BC, where the thrones
met the saints and the prophets. I mean the Roman Emperors
bent the Christian details to gain the wealth of the people's love
of astrologers. The first empirical data. These days Pfizer does
a six week trial and we call it truth but 700 years the Sumerians
documented the position of Saturn and the price of wheat and
it's habernacky to us. What on earth do you put faith in my dear?
I would say beyond earth but I presume you are a dialectical
materialist like your good Marxist politics. As my dear French
father said, "you think you are an atheist, but everyone has faith
in something, be it electricity or that god does not exist." That
might be slightly holistic for your set theory which holistically
avoids the holistic, but I'll gladly hear the counter example.
Where was your tipping point for belief? I suppose it was years
of thought, but there must be a fall off the seesaw you want to tell
me about.

I wonder, why a doctrine? Even if you win History, that
unattainable virgin, you'll spend eternity with the maggots, the
fact-mongerers typing away at your flesh. I suppose you don't
mind contributing to humanity, just a bone left, a truism in the
end. But would it have been any different otherwise? Personally,
I'm leaving only ashes. Burnt pages. Not deconstruction. Pure
flame. You philosophers are made of metal, but I am earth water
fire. The triskelion. Horned and abandoned. Who wants the
power of the name if it's only to claim your own bullseye? Already
got it plenty, darts, doin just fine.

Well it's sassy time tonight, yes, agreed. Your logic's got me all
bunched like a rolled sleeve. It's fine enough on its own, but
against my wrinkles and veins and memories something else

has to course against the grain. There's so many of you, arguing your details since the beginning of time, screw it, I want a literary song. Unwind the arguments because I was never that great at compartments, and when I was, it didn't get me laid. Philosophy is all moral consequence and politics, real time. Miserably. Your set theory has no "I", so Houdini!, but subject object event gets back to the sun eventually. You hide in math. I hide in the moon. And I only ask you this, if e to the negative two pi i contains all the numbers we have never seen but that make the circle, the financial world and the imaginary realm all come together to equal one, then you must believe in things we cannot see or touch or feel but only believe.

All the artists I know know this: closest thing I've got to reason is the voice in my head. None of us can see that. Here's the voice in my head. Here it is. I made it prettier for you but it's what I think. I guess the difference between you and me is that I only trade my voice with you. Maybe you spent all those years making your voice for everyone, as round and flat and true as everything. Oh, a metaphor about our work. I just wish I could hear your voice. The one in your head.

Yours, Katy

Dear Alain,

My father told me my project to write you love letters was creepy. I said, imagination and hope are elements as real as the table before your eyes! Imagine father!

A la prochaine, Kati

Dear Alain,

I'm going to have to get back to the intangible soon. I think you like real numbers, but I prefer the imaginary; the i. The square root of negative one, that is. Can you see it? You must be a genius.

xo, k

Dear Alain,

My new roommate Brandon is a found poem. I like it. When I think of all the things I don't have time to be nostalgic for I feel irresponsible. It makes me care about the heart more than being smart. It is not that time is a mirage, but that it's a villain and I am consensually guilty of moving on. There's no grammar around that. Just hiding from the images that bring us most comfort.

We long for revolution, but I have been there and all that's fought for is the peace to enjoy the apple on the worn wood table. It's folksy to center the flowers in their vase, simple and symmetrical, but I'll still call it beautiful for my Ma. Do you mind?

Yours, Katy

Dear Alain,

The past few weeks...well I passed out at the office yesterday
and think it might be from stress. My boss rode me like an
investment banker, I was sick. I was up for promotion, he was up
for promotion. I got news my friend died, I had a job interview
the next day. I reconnected with high school friends, I made a
memorial fund. I got sicker. There were 4,000 poets in my city
for a conference, I had five days and ten events. I didn't get the
job. My mother was diagnosed with a derivative of tuberculosis.
I tried to quit smoking. Oh yea, it was the Egyptian revolution. I
watched Al Jazeera constantly and cried at the beauty of belief in
the impossible.

And all I can think about is our parallel lines meeting. Tell me you
believe in love.

Yours,
Katy

Into the streets of Cairo

Go to every door

Tell them to come out tomorrow

We will not go home

Dear Alain,

I love you more than ever. You wrote that the Tunisian and Egyptian uprisings have a universal significance. They prescribe new possibilities whose value is international.

I could not agree more. When Mubarak finally stepped down, I was just headed from my office to lunch. I stepped outside to consider the importance of this revolution, this televised moment of history as important as, the paris commune or the french revolution or, or, as important as, Tahrir itself. Tahrir means To Freedom, literally, or, independence as I'm sure you know. And as I stepped out outside on the street I began to sob. I really did. I was crying on the street and thought, perhaps you look a little silly on the street here, so I went to the bookstore where my friend Rod works. I cried more at the bookstore. All in all it took about two hours to exhaust myself of the tears and I am not sure anyone really understood - most people just think I'm overly emotional or maybe crazy - but I cried because I am not crazy and Egypt proves it. That moment when he left, when Mubarak left through peaceful means, through universal, peaceful spontaneous, beautiful power of the people, it's, it's every single person in the world who said "things can be better", it's every single person in the world who dared to say "torture is wrong", it's every single person who dared to dream, it's every single person who went to sleep with hope for a better future, it's every single ignorant fucking imbecile who only said "no" going to hell, it's everyone who called me crazy for hoping, for believing, for wanting more, it's to hell with them, and it was worth it, it was all worth it, it was true, it is possible, it was worth the sacrifice it is all worthwhile we can and the big words are worth a damn and I cried and cried and cried because all the idealism was true and all the blood and the bruises and the torture was losing, it wasn't structure anymore, it was a tall building made of electric fence for everyone to hail with bruises and scars and untouchables, that facade collapsed, and there was a sun to heal the scars, and the romance of poetry survives and this is why I cried: for all the pain of anyone who ever said "I guess that's how it has to be" because it didn't have to be that way the day Mubarak left, it was singing and dancing in the street among all the people, it was the resounding ring of the subtle non-violent line, it was the rise out of silence of the truth, that magic of the white dove from the darkest, gentleman's top hat, the scar become the badge, the tear become the holy water, the transcendence, the moment where the best side of humanity came true, and everything we write for, everything we live for, everything we ever dared to believe was worth it all.

PS. It's parallel lines meeting at infinity. It's when Gauss looked at the horizon and said, but parallel lines do meet, they meet at the horizon. It's the dream of the platonic form lapping at the edge of the shore and the tide rushing over one last time to a blazing red dawn, the kind that makes you wake up and breathe as if for the first time and all those tones of sarcasm fade into some jellyfish dying on the sand and it's blindingly beautiful the stuff we always knew was there but just grew too cynical to care except maybe deep in the night we risked a word or two of "maybe" and "i hope" and "it still is" and "there is more" and we dreamed and we dreamed and we dreamed and it was the real projective plane and things do happen at infinity and i still believe in love and i'm getting on a plane because i believe that if the egyptians can then why not, we can have it too. i still believe.

I love you.

Bisous.

Dear Alain,

I'm not here to elaborate on your experience, I'm here to remind you of your soul.

K

"Love is nothing other than a trying sequence of
investigations on the disjunction and the Two." – A.B.

$$k_1 + \alpha_1$$

"Love is interminable fidelity to the first declaration." – A.B.

Dear Alain,

I've fallen into unrequited love again. There's nothing that makes me more fun to be around.

Yrs,
Katy

Dear Alain,

The problem ultimately is that to define anything is to take a position of power. Are you comfortable with your power? I hate power. I refuse to define. I refuse it. I refuse to be powerful, I refuse to make sense, I refuse I refuse. I refuse in protest. I'm a soft, silly, wild flower basket of love. All I see is your ego and I'm going to stuff a chalky powder comment in the cracks, because I hate power. My mission is to dissolve it. But of course, this is my deepest secret I reveal to you! My deepest secret because to name a mission is itself to have power – don't you see? I don't give a damn I forgive you always! What, rules? What rules? They're power. They're cultural sets for specific power layers, they're always false when turned over or meshed. Fuck them. You need something? You need to know you're important? You are. Does your power put things in jeopardy? Always. Do I forgive you? I don't even have a choice. I am a poet. I have no power. I have nothing. I am water. I know love. I give everything your psyche needs; I take nothing. No story, no moment of self, no words of self. Some babble if your ego needs.

Dear Alain,

Here are two concepts that give me a headache: Revolution and infinity. By comparison, even God seems a clear-cut conundrum.

You seem to be the set of all sets, Alain. What say you?

Dear Alain,

These letters are just shit. I'm only writing them because the literati will eat them. Mange-le. I know.

I know. But the truth is power. Is lines in the sand and you know the bloom doesn't come from lines. Political events cannot be quantified. You said it. Page 7, 32, 45, 66-69, 98-100, XYZ... J, K, W, Politics and Metaphysics. Definitions, blah blah blah. Who cares about categories when there's death by dehydration? The bloom Alain, I'm talking about the bloom!

Tais-Toi!

I'm going to melt you

PS it's more than form, it's more than Mallarme, it's underneath...

Dear Alain,

Your shoulder blades the shimmer of molten silver.

Oh Alain!

It's trust dripping down to the ground, or where the ground used to exist!

Dear Alain,

I want to see you, ie fuck you and then later, make love to you very much. My desire for you is so strong it won't let me go; it scares me; it makes me weep.

I've been very even keeled the past while. The intensity is back, with you. Now. I'm not sure either one of us wants that kind of Katy insanity but I would be crazy for you this weekend.

I really am not being dramatic, please, believe me. I'm weeping honesty because there is no other choice.

Please do the right thing for both of us. It's just a question if you feel this same intensity: we would work the rest out or break our hearts trying. Or I would, again.

For you,
K

Alain,

The key is to understand that no one will ever "get" you. It's impossible. To remember that, hurts, a lot. So we lie to ourselves or, if we're smart, we take affection where we can get it. It's just mirrors and smoke dancing around a big void. If we're lucky, we have a lot of mirrors and plenty of smoke and even get a glimpse of the black hole once or twice to remind us to keep smiling, because, we can.

Dear Alain,

Well, as you know I'm a juvenile stuck on the problem of naming. So I've gone to the source, addicted to sex and obsessed with sounds, sensations, feelings. You claim naming was solved by some anti-naming mechanism. Theorizing the naming into some other system. But I'm done with concrete! Eww. Put it in a bottle throw it out to sea. Your systems don't give a damn for psyche. I want them destroyed completely. I want to drown. What do you say of philosophy to a Chinese woman who has never used a personal pronoun but who knows her master's name, with glee! She giggles!

I'm going under now – come with me...

How can you talk about these things mechanically? As if philosophy were as binary and blameless as a lightswitch? These are human beings and their thoughts their hearts their messy souls. Multiplicity is generous but are you God? Do you judge? Oh I could scream! I just want to save them all, all 7.22 Billion from your arrogance.

Oh but you poor baby, you do, you work. It's born of generosity and you have seen the source, it's the events of Robespierre, not Kant's assessment. Laundry clean smelling despite the shit stains. Perhaps because. You try. I understand. But I would commit suicide before I would write a single word of, for, and, about, under, within, on top, above, below or anywhere around a human mind, I wouldn't name a single one thing – it claims too much! And yet I dare do exactly that to you – you are just as guilty of your fate as any! And pain, you must know pain, who doesn't? And if you don't, god bless you!

Oh human being, my beloved human being!

Dear Alain,

Power is all in our heads these days. Where is the magical green grass? Plain electrons aren't so colorful. Green lights of google chat, be my disco ball!

Holding my heart for your quantum, beyond the boring binary.

Yours, always,
Kati

My dear,

I would love you any way, you are the least offensive of the crowd. None of us are innocent. Except perhaps my mother. All ways are less of more and in that way of course, more.

Is that poetry? Does it grasp at beyond? I am. Swingin' anyway. At bat. & the skies are blue.

Love, K

PS. I know, I know. It's all contained in multiplicity. But what of synchronicity? You said infinity? But what of the irrational?

Dear Alain,

Just that disagreement can be more intimate than "yea, I know
me too" and the gulf between us fills me more than your cock;
pushed up against my wall, the gulf between us daring me to fall,
right into the embrace of your views. Wrong. I'm playing hard to
get; come here. Now. I was sweet enough to show you where to
climb. My nipples, hard.

Yes you're lacking introspection to a fault and I am swelling with
the lyric I but don't tell me you're somehow less self-involved
you with your adoration of intellectual porn, false precision
and smooth façade. Yes you indulge in grey antique moments
of stolen admiration for the reflective mind, but this is rap for
academics, and we've the same ambivalent hard-on for theory
though it too exclusive for our political proclamations and we're
full of fancy martinis our hearts love but somehow don't satisfy
the romantic aluminum can of our peasant cornfield dreams.
We're filled with contradiction, and so are you, despite your
proclamations of sympathy, tender otherness and sensuality as
non-political dream moment. It's true past the judgment, ticket
in, whatever tribal proclamation inherited, developed or inverted.
We have to chose somehow, ought it be a common language

ni hui ying yu ma?

Could you love that other? Could I love without "I"? Could it be a
breath suspended by the challenge of the gulf?

53

Dear Alain,

I'm an unbiased weirdo and everything around me is a big
unbiased joke. Forgive my harsh words. I want you. I love you.
Come back to me.

Hard stop at irreducible.

k

You say, Alain, that Mallarme, who thinks nothing but is pure form is the epitome of poesie. But you're dead wrong. The poet is who does the terrible task of ranking love, the anchor to your symphony, without which you are merely erection. In short, I am too good for you.

A dieu,
Kati

ARE YOU FUCKING KIDDING ME ALAIN? LOOK YOU FUCKING TOAD, I TOOK ABSTRACT ALGEBRA. I HAVE A DEGREE IN PURE MATHEMATICS, AND I'M FUCKING TELLING YOU, LOGIC ISN'T EVERYTHING. DON'T TELL ME IM BEING BLOODY IRRATIONAL, YOU GODDAMN DENSE ACADEMIC. I'M LEAVING. DOES IT HURT NOW? IS THAT REAL? WHERE IS THE TIMELESS HEART IS IN YOUR STUPID FUCKING SET THEORY? CIRCUBSCRIBE THAT YOU FRENCH TOAD.

FUCKER.

YOU COULD ONLY LOVE A SQUARE.

LITERALLY.

Affair #2

Slavoj,

How lovely to meet another Slovene here in New York. A rarity indeed, and you

are delectable.

Drinks, tomorrow? I'll bring my earplugs.

X, k

Alain,

If the superficial is all irrelevant in the face of love then who gives a damn about form anyway. I mean, yea, poets aren't supposed to work out but can you still hate my tight thighs for provoking what ain't real love just lust? Not sayin, just sayin. I mean, what does that matter in the middle of the sea except you're drowning and I'm kicking. Yea. I'm kicking. So yea. Whatever. It's all just set theory anyway.

PS I'm busy. I gave you my under but you could not understand it. It is not understandable. You couldn't see my psyche kneeling on the floor? Swimming in an ancient song of Sappho? It's not a poem. It's where poems spring from, dear.

Alain,

Dear. It's not exactly in the moment of the Greeks. I use this as a directionality to point you towards the fact that the sensation is not of this time. It is not in fact, of any time. It is a place where time does not exist, or even words, only perhaps contradiction or a slow lethargy. It's rather unnamable, really. If you don't sense it, you don't sense it. That's all, really. Sorry.

Cheers, K

Dear Diary,

Choosing between the collection of afterthoughts and the tautology of conjunct tautologies.

I want the swimming pool. All these pricks can do is pose and posture. That's it?

Julian...no he can't let go. Someone will snipe him.

Xo, me

The thing is, Alain, you can know everything a person thinks and still have no idea what they're thinking.

Dear Diary,

Of course he returns! Now, that I've turned my head!
How logical --

x, k

Dear Alain,

I suppose you've mapped sociality like a chessboard. But I'm mercurial, at best. A single phrase - energy illuminations. I'm addicted! I worry not because things won't be alright, but because things won't be perfect. I worry we'll seep apart. Not our legs or minds, our souls, dusty with un-worried un-care. After a million days dust becomes a chemical thick compound coating ancient cave paintings filmed polysyllabic by Herzog. Worry is cleaning our etchings. Pay attention. Feed us always. So we aren't a museum, but always real. I know I shouldn't use that word. I'm dusting us. Because I care. Because I love you.

Love,

Me

I am here to ask for your protection. To provide space for my attempts at the avant garde. My future does not look like yours. My future looks like hurricanes and tornados and mass displacement. And if not mine then my children's, certainly. I don't have time to consider the timeless future of modernity's progress. I wish I had the strength of Pythagoras and the Gods of Achilles to dream into the horizon as you do. I love your work. I admire its beauty. You are the horizon, infinite. Golden on silver shimmer.

But I have to think of what we might preserve. I plan for what should be remembered; what values; what vibrations of harmony and love need float when apocalypse hell comes for the children.

Simplistic and provincial. What would the future be without provincial? It's as idyllic as anything. You are, I communicate. That is the difference. I am asking for your protection. Not from the people but so I may go to the people. Humbly, I hope you will consider my request

With all due respect

With all due respect of work thought, imagined, forged and impassioned. Do not regret your beliefs now. Work is work. And all work for all segments is equally valid. Protect me as your own or show the true ranking you believe in: one is better. I do not want to corner you, but must. Do you only believe in the best, or do you believe in all who work?

Love, Katy

Slavoj, darling,

I must send my regrets. I'm missing my earplugs, so I can't make it tonight. I hope your flight back tomorrow will be safe, swift, and in first class so – not a chatty annoyance around.

Your brilliance sparkles too too much for mere mortals! Dommage, le coco n'est pas possible cette fois. A la Slovenie !

Poslovite!

Dear Alain,

Meow. Come, be cliché. Square checked placemat, the table set for two, candlesticks sans cobwebs, crystalline sweet peas. Nonsense poignantly gestured across the universe, en français des siècles, not Napoleon or la cimetière but ours. Whiskey, or wine. Your mind against mine. Nonsense when the gulf chasms. Softly, where the wet gathers. Hard into the under. Worlds open where our lips meet. This you feel. Come inside to the nothing-everything.

Philosophers of your generosity should breathe multiplicity. The Greeks believed that beginning with Eros led to hell. I think of Juarez. It was Agape, Philia, then Eros the ideal. We have all three. Come, tonight!

x.

Dear Alain,

That was good.

Lv, k

Dear Alain,

For you, baby? Rules.

1. Avoid the void.
2. Always act to preserve and maximize the other's psyche.
3. I tell you how I feel, you console me, I wet, we make love.

Oh, and please be on time.

What else is there?

love, k

ps, A, 69 pages~

Dear Alain,

Your own rules irk you? Touché. I enjoy the less structured anyway. Shall you admit 50 shades of capitalism, S&M, Sartre? Isn't philosophy a scheduled distribution of power?

Sorry, I'll be good.

They say in the next life the philosopher is a dancer. I say in the next life the poet is a janitor. Will you come with me?

I'm with whiskey. Would you like some?

Love,

"There is some sense in Plato's project of crowning the poets in order to send them to exile...It is because poetry propagates the idea of an intuition of the nothing." – A.B.

$$k_2 + \alpha_2$$

"My soul cannot be the object of my judgment and knowledge; much more are my judgment and knowledge the objects of my soul." – Carl Jung

Alain, dearest,

I know we can't say these things out loud because love is best a secret. But this is a letter. I know how you like it. and why. Because the terror and pain of the world are so great, we owe it to be peaceful and beautiful aesthetically and never say a foul-toned word. replace with (owe is not the word but there is no word for this kind of required giving) but Opposition? to be a monk.

You fair well. You write constructively in an age of deconstructive destruction, a beach ball on Omaha Beach. Where once there was blood and ocean. Bastions and leagues. What you fear I will say is that I am the ocean and blood.

Love is thinking for two (+). The world is multiplicity. You grow our views towards the best of mathematics: structure, order to embrace and sustain a peace where violence isn't necessary and terror isn't known, and we can drink table wine, goat cheese, gruyere, tarte au framboise, tartare au boeuf con salade, des crepes, comme ca. Work in peace, all in peace and plenty in a life idyllic until the Utopia arrives we resist by being these things to preserve them. We are what we wish would be because if we aren't they will disappear. And who will know after the Reckoning what to strive for, what to fight for, what to preserve if no one remembers what love is? It's a bourgeois sensibility: honesty, sweetness, simplicity, calm, small things. Greatness in small things. Because hell, gentle should be the normative state! And anyone who would smash down with wagging finger and drooling spit-up "rar how boring" well how then, without the small, should Marxist society converge to thrive? I'd like to see it work without honesty and generosity. We'd all steal each other's rice. Moreover, for those who fight and fight and fight for the space to breathe! We must fight for them but we must not complain at what we enjoy. Imagine how crass! Stand next to the man who has nothing and tell him how terrible your life is. How terrible your iPhone and nearly brand new clothes you got at the thrift store for an hour's work. Say it out loud? Yes. Structurally abysmal. And abysmally worse for many. But

Joie de Vivre must live! Gratitude must live! Those without say, if I may not, may you. And we must, for them, remember the stars are free for all.

The real is what we need if everything is gone.

Dear Alain,

I thought we were talking about how i relate to the movie. but
alas...it becomes something else, a philosophy that is above
my head. Though I do try. Yes, the letters are false. They are an
artifice. It's a romance novel of a sort. Aware of itself and self-
critical of its selfness. You're right. I'm terrible at life because I
am, too political. Very much so. Poetry is, as you say, my attempt
to escape. I loathe the political view, because, it is terribly tedious.
Terribly so. As for believe versus imagine...yes i am an idealistic
nincompoop. i wont let go of the rubric.

The rubric, by the way, is never break a heart.

Yours, K

Well Alain,

You are the man of multiplicity. I suppose I assumed you wanted to learn my singularity.

K

Oh you want me to speak of "my true inner self". Well my "true inner self" is composed of a catalogue of failures. My "self", my lesser self, is full of the small delights I take in refusing myself those failures. I suppose you can choose which you prefer.

xo, k

Dear Alain,

I always feel a glow, the best, when I confess to you and you say
"no" and explain to me why I'm wrong. There's there there. It's
the last thing. Integrity of learning. It's not commodified. No
power. No help or hospitality, a glow.

Dear Alain,

We talk every day. But late in the idle evening, so rarely it comes,
a blue moon, I consider how you course through my veins. I think
history is a sensation I feel when suspended from mundanity in
change. An aeroplane completely alone in my head. Life is worry,
trivial, he said she said, gossip and details. History the prism
flying into the next phase of a consideration. Fate on a graham
cracker. Don't ask me why. It's life in a freezer. Stolen from the
bliss of simplicity.

Importance an oil rig jigged up by the media. Dunno a poetic
term for media. Clowns would be excruciatingly polite. So banal
to speak of the evil, I'm embarrassed for Hannah Arendt to invoke
her saying.

But that's power. So I redefine it. I love my friends. That's it.

Charles Olson interests me. Meg Ronan read him in my bathtub
once. It was annoying at the time, was tired, wanted to sleep.
But of course now, among my favorite moments. Profoundly
unprofound. You know, lovely. Well, it was also glamorous as hell.
But the profound moments are necessarily contaminated. This
was cooking and nothing-everything.

So, poetry in a bathtub...

Yours,
K

Dear Alain,

Uhg. What's wrong? Le monde. Let's move to a cave in Nepal. No. To a desert in Addis. No somewhere less cliché. Let's ascribe meaning based on what a small set of relatively meaningless but self-important people proclaim to be relatively bougie. So no, we can't move to a cave in Nepal. A hole on Mars? That's so outré in New York. So unmeaninged and escapable. Let's write and write and write to create new layers of meaningless escape from what has become our most recently meaninged hell. Away with us. Let's go.

No emotions here.
K

Alain,

Sure, whatever tautology you said-not said. Yes, right, I'm being a snarky sarcastic bitch, impossible to connect with. Sure. What you said, lonely.

K

Yes sir.

No it's not yes sir. It's everything. Life, life, we could do so much for each other and we sit around playing power games of suck who's dick and when and how and how long and don't say anything and you have but I don't and there is never any sense of ok, I'm here, it's ok exactly as it is and sure let's share and be peaceful. Society is a race of gain to offset loss, which is greater, and worse and never discussed and compassion considered a crime of the weak. My fucking god. I know you think this too, we're lefties, and then we all go do lefty things and treat each other like republicans. It's an act. An act of art to devote oneself to mercy and I've devoted myself to you, and you are the only one I can write to, can be so honest with. I'm going to try not to fear to lose this but just be grateful that it is and is now and has been at some point and thank this life for the miracle of that. Wonder. Wonder is the only thing that gets me by. I have no idea how you live without Hallmark Cards. Well, your theory on love, I must be honest is. It is dear. What of love of one for three? Or love of one for n+1? Agape. Yes. Hehe. No not like that, you boy. Interminable! You see this conversation is literally a mold. Ready made. I'm not bored though. How could I reject all 99 per-zillion-per-cent of the conversers? Actually, it's just my local community at this point in time-space I would reject. The serious-girl comment follow boy joke follow girl eeeeee. Cave men? The universal "we're on equal planes"? Who all does it mean what to and when and where? I give up. The point is, the point was, Hallmark Cards. Because I'm saying, I love them. Patterns. I don't love asymmetry. I stand and stare, etc. But I don't love it. How could I feel anything at all? It doesn't remind me of anything? Bah the derivative hole. The derivative hole. Want New to escape, take the derivative until it gets to the irreducible form. Repeat with varying polynomials. Singularity. Art. Philosophy. Derivative hole. I don't think it's a coincidence that in English derivative is a dirty word. Derrida collapsed the derivatives market. I know, it's hysterical, isn't it. My dear, I'm going to really insult you now, but I think you've become integral. As have I. You said it's the look in Robespierre's eye that births philosophy. It's true. Empiricism. Empiricism's relationship to Empire? Integral. Art, derivative. Why do I insult you? Why do you like it? It's so formulaic. You like formulas, I know. So you can think. I know. Me too.

Goodnight,
k

Obsessed? Oh yes. I'm rather evangelical about it. I'm sure you've found my pattern by now. It's computers and the lack of empathy. Lack of hospitality of a relatively secure society. Contrary, where tragedy has been humans learn to share. Where I grew up its buy buy buy mine mine mine. They say it's the marketing, and sure, but it's also stability. Thus, over-built structure. Buying is a clean line in the sand. Who helps is a debt to repay. Where everyone's in debt up to their cultural revolutionary gut baskets, why keep track? Just help. Know pain? Know giving in equal measure, if you've known love. Always offer food. Ni chi le ma? Simple. Love is simple too. Give because it's the human thing to do. The ones who don't know what love is. More these days. More Juarez. More Camden. More me being evangelical.

Oh my joke is crass, huh? That's not what you said the other night, tadpole. No, you look like a tadpole when you sleep. Thought, I like it fine. But images and feelings, the transitory. There's too much wrong with thought. It's too limited. It's spherical and impossible. The moment is total in my typewriter, sweet cheeks. As are you. When will the teasing unspool? I'm free tonight.

"The poem must be excused, the argument must be praised." – A.B.

$$k_3 + \alpha_3$$

" 'Philosphers', says Rimbaud, 'You belong to your West' " – A.B.

Alain,

Everything OK, integral?

X, k

Dear Diary,

The letters fall off. Busy. Fine. One day. Be sated with the thing itself. Always something more. Timbuktu, money, fame. A thought process. How conscious. A chapter titled "Infinity and End of Romanticism". Aiyaiyai

I'm a poet mathematics IS the beginning of romanticism! sigh.

New age, or brooklynite, or elite to believe?

Don't, don't even utter such stupid words. It is the modern who fail to believe.

X

Dear Alain,

What's wrong?! Venus in the 5th house. Ascendant in Gemini
conjunct North Node conjunct Transit of Venus 2004 and 2012.
Helen of Troy. Hera dethroned. Etc. Thought trails phenomena.
You ride. I drag. Choices we've made. You are lucky, dear, that you
don't work with vibe. Non-thought for you is thought, or, non-
thought. Math. I'm an Eskimo on snow re: non-thought. 50 words
for intuition: self-catalogued. Not crazy. Convinced. Love, Jung.
Defender. Etc. Etc.

Yours,
k

Heroin? I wish. I'd probably be a better writer.

What are you doing to keep you from me?

Oh you want to know what I think now? Oh dear. How shall I put this? In a poem, in play, in a math proof?

Well you see my dear, I love your set theory. So I'll use that. I think that philosophy is the set of all possible thoughts. But not just thoughts today, but thoughts from all parts of human history. You see, I love your work, but to be honest it's too linear for me. It moves in one direction. This is how you say things like "the end of romanticism", as if romanticism is something past. The truth is, first, that philosophy is the set of all possible perspectives, but not just from this moment in time, but from all moments in time.

I think if philosophy, your definition, is expanded to this definition than so many other thoughts are incorporated and included. Freudian psychology is one example. For what is Freud except the attempt to explain that the mind is not just affected by the present but also the past. He writes of it as if it's mother father playing games with us, but it's saying at base, I think, that our histories are our presents, much as we modern's would prefer to ignore the jests of our pasts.

The design of forgetting the past is so Western Colonial tension to me. And it's not that progress and new forms are in any way subordinate to old forms, but I don't think old forms can be escaped. Even the new form is running from the old form and so in this way is affected by it, for what is the new form without the presence of the old form? The two may be disjunct but they would not exist without each other.

And also, you see the way I conceive of the world is at once traditional and modern. I am creating something new but it builds on the past to embrace the future and the traditional. I like Gauss' projective plane. There infinity is the just horizon but it is also right now. Which is to say that thought and being are not just points on a directional linear trajectory, but that they are sort of a collection of moments which circle back into a complete thing, like a mobius strip no one point being predominant over the other. You might say birth or death begins or ends, but a beginning or an ending do not presuppose directionality in a circle. There are many forms of thought which support the circle view, Hinduism, Eastern concepts of reincarnation, Alzheimer's disease. And to circle back, saying philosophy is the set of all thoughts ever and everywhere, expands on your multiplicity of possible events to go even further to discuss the multiplicity of all possible thoughts and thought systems.

The beauty of this is that it solves the problem of post-colonialism. Which is not just a problem, but a reality. How else does any philosophy not become just a competitor to say an East African tribal thought. They are all philosophy and all truth, to someone. But regional or historical.

But I also believe that thought from all parts of history are valid. To many, there are forms of thought which are distinctly invalid. Thus, the question of evil.

But you see, and I'm getting excited now, the most beautiful thing is that if you follow this logic and use your definition of the New God, as you call it, as some external, unlimited infinity, but you work in the system of Gauss' Projective Plane, then God becomes not something external but exactly being or humanity or the point – the experience – itself. Because we are the infinite plane. Everything alive is the infinite plane. We are limitless. And each moment that occurs is a conjunction of instances, a moment of infinity. Thus each moment of being is God, and the collection of these moments is Being. It's not that we are God. It's that existence itself is God, and as all moments are multiple and infinitely possible and happening, God is infinite. But not outside. Here, itself! Like you said!

Oh but my dear, what would I do? Go to conferences? They'd never - I don't have a PhD. And what of my tone! It's much, much too sweet.

Why does serious have to come in the tone of a math professor? Are you serious? Come on. Think a little bit, would you?

Valid and real. Think about the words you're using!

No, I can't. I was made to play in the fields. And besides. Western philosophy, the entire corpus of it would never. The line of the mother made its way to ingrained. It's just Christianity and Abraham in a straight line. Live in a circle I say. Listen! Central asian thinkers – Persian or Afghani or whereever depending on the nation state point in time – and then the Frenchies, and a bajillion more Hindus. But we are always reduced to poets or others. Maybe if I write it in math you will fuck me, but sigh that's probably it. An old idea made new, and still in their same old prisons. Again and again. Dictatorship of the moderns. Although, Gauss was very revolutionary. And besides, where would I preach from, the potty?

No of course you should still use the real projective plane.

I'm not saying you're not the set of all sets Alain. Just go up a field. It's ok to be a subset!

But seriously, if it's not for them, it's not universal. I pray to you now. You are what articulates my beliefs, to a large degree. But I speak your Western language. What about those who pray to Guenon, or Sol, or Sadiq Jalal Al Azm, or Massignon, or Emperor Khosrau? Does it matter what if it's the event without anxiety?

Let's just go to live by the sea. Forget all these overblown beehives and dissolve. It would be so modern to forget everything and swim in the lightness of being.

That IS the revolution, Alain.

FINE I'LL USE THE HARSHER TONES.

YOU ARE SO UGLY.

Just don't ever tell me there's no power in what you do. You are tall, strong man who uses serious tones – but don't ever tell me there's no power in the presentation. I know all about form, buddy.

And let me get this straight. Slavoj Zizek is the best, but you're accusing me of contradicting myself? Um human being versus computers... PS Heraclitus?

And I don't hate modernism! It's just singularity... Multiplicity you baguette!

Dear Alain,

I'm so sorry. I'm so sorry to be always screaming at you. I realize it is not you I'm mad at, but philosophy.

I've just finished "Philosophy and Desire". I was wet the whole time – no, I'm kidding. It's much more serious than that.

You see I was once Robespierre. I don't know how to say this.

I was in China working for the Revolutionary movement. Competing narratives everywhere and threat to life – mine and hundred thousands millions more. The Chinese government say X is true. The individual wakes up one morning and says Goddamn Y is true. He resists. His wife and family are killed. It's tragic.

All these people daring to stand up and say – no! Y is true! Screw you lying government! And sometimes Y is true only because a single word is there to stand on. Imagine if all these people were plagued by the Derridian, well the word might actually be $z, z_1, z_2, z_3, z_4 \ldots z_{n+1}$. How would they ever stand?

Hell. Derrida is hell.

I know because I did it myself. In the end I had to say, I am a singular soul. I am the unique set off all my experiences and I say Y is true and that is all there is.

Fuck Derrida. I'm sorry to hate but he abandoned me. And everyone else except the armchairs. Comfortable cock diddlers.

You. You do not. You write with your heart for "them" not "them". You write for the ones who need something to stand on.

I was a broken Heideggerian poem after all of them. But you. I love you, Alain.

Yours, always,
Katy

I love you too. My integral, my builder, my man –

Happy moments do happen, Alain. We must build them every day, as much as we can.

Fine. Use field theory. Whatever. Real projective plane is poetic. I know you aren't above poetic tricks, Alain. But yes, the math is difficult. They can all meet at the projective plane. One day.

And my tone? I'm flirting with you, Rabat. To be honest, for all your multiplicity, I'm surprised no one has accused you of being an Islamist yet.

I'm beginning to think that in this fragile world of ours it is revolutionary merely to pass a moment of joy. I worry it will dissolve in all this violence, this capitalism, this displacement. If the truth is a hole, I'm hardly after it. I want to breathe the joy back into it.

I fear we'll forget what it is. And then, what will there be then?

Why? I do, of course. I know the process of love is thought, but what is IT? I just know. There's something before the process, a spark, an intuition, a capacity, a talent, an intangible variable, an energy, an attraction, a fate, a folly, a falling, a poem.

More and more you are all I think of. More and more I become you. Look at my language! More you less me. I'm sure you throw some nouns around for the sound of it that you maybe didn't before. But that's process. What is, IT?

I may fail in the process, but I do love you.

Yrs,

Childish awe. Womb where the womb is nine months of day dream. Not dripping. Contained. Voidish, you little slut, come here. Ice cubes in cocktails, heavy. Shots if you will but I think they burn. Small in the naval. A knuckle I didn't let go of. Dalmatian cigarettes. The only thing that's formless is God.

"Little by little the contour of a subset of the situation is outlined, in which the eventual axioms of the truth are verified." – A.B.

$$k_n + a_n$$

"The subject of a truth demands the indiscernible." – A.B

I'm floating.

Two parallel lines meet. Alain, at the horizon.

Hose Maria Penãta once said to me: leprechauns are the worst kind of enemy. I didn't know it at the time, but he was right. At the time, I thought he was crazy. Leprechauns? Who believes in leprechauns these days? The foolish and the short-sighted, the dreamers and the failures, the peaceful ones whose time strokes the sidewalks like the lull of a back-porch rocking chair.

Penãta was married to a lovely, stout lady named Henretta, not only for her attention to all the details he never imagined, but mostly for the way her surety popped like lazy eggs on a fryer. Once they abandoned the city for a shiny shack with some grass, Henretta made those eggs too, in the kitchen next to the porch while Penãta read the paper on his rocker. Henretta wore an apron stained with greasy time, and articulated her body in swift, short strokes of authority. Penãta listened to her move without realizing it, as he dreamed about the histories long forgotten by the practicalities of daily life. It was a quaint existence, one that permitted the rhythms of time to discuss themselves at length, humming along persistently in ample fashion, taking up the day like a child's awareness of sunshine or rainstorms, a kind of quiet and amused prayer about the simple things in life. Like the beauty of passing time in silent observation.

Q.E.D.

Dear Alain,

Eventually I'll have to leave. There are no words for why. It's
not an event and it's not a death. There is nothing I can say to
reassure you. There is nothing I can say to reassure myself. There
are no words. I just, I can't be here. I belong, somewhere else.

I will love you.
Always.

I'm sorry.

Well then put me back the way Heidegger had us. Dissolve into me!

I don't think so, anymore.

Do you want to hear the wretched tone of grief?

How else am I going to drag us out of this hell, unless I pretend it doesn't exist?

Huh, Plato?

And I take your hand in the air. I sing in your ear. We dance, just an awkward little thing enough to have you in my arms and the warmth is enough to banish it all.

Later it's enough to buoy some mathematics. Peaceful thought sans consequence. Being qua being. I consider that if some exist with emotional reactions to numbers, ethical considerations for primes and perfect squares, then math is no longer peaceful. Irrational numbers the imperfect terrible deriddian drain post-modern hell. Inescapable. Platonic form a dog toy we perpetually reach up for only for the wretched owners to pull it away and laugh isn't that dog cute doesn't he love to play?

Everyone likes to think they aren't a crazy lover but the truth is im fragile broken and crying too. The movements I can't bear break me I've been forever broken since. You never broke. Or your shatter was never to break again, to sew it all together. Stitch by precious word. Stitch. O the tapestry you built. A blanket to shelter every soul. And they broke into sticks, poking holes to see the wretched sky. Stars. Weeping through the architecture. Willows fucking in the grass. Poppies on dollars and pipes. Pied. Termites. Loathful eating again into grace dissolution the sea the sound under water the empty push of tears birthing. Dying on your cheeks a tome written there rosetta stone cold iteration endurance $n+1$ to infinity where all parallel lines meet not in our minds in Gauss at the horizon in Revolution in every moment in every moment at every moment ever in pure love

We meet at infinity

"The sadness of the true changes into the joy of being when seen from close up." – A.B.

$$k_{n+1} + \alpha_{n+1}$$

"Who is not familiar with the tiresome exhaustion of such refutations, which can be summed up by the deplorable syntagm 'you do not understand me'? An enervated form, we might say, of the declaration of love. Who loves well understands poorly." – A.B.

Dear Alain,

So, I know historicism isn't "true" and this is different from saying history isn't true – right? So I'll say a thing again about "this time". Apocalyptic scenarios abound and we've seen periods of this before, through-out, all over, forget China, I mean the collapse of the entire Western Cannon. We'll see about "post" when the Chinese re-write history in their totalitarian likeness. How's that PhD going for you? Orientalism a best-seller, the edited version. It is silly to judge but I will tell you in my love letter, if China takes over, if the places of free speech dim their lights one by one and the smog greys my tears...

Anyway, too much for me, I'm going back to stupidity, seriously. I've been investigating small details with the fervor of a child's fist over candy. It's the only thing makes my brain race again, frolic really, in cinematic green fields where there are no thorns just a canopy of apple blossoms.

Do you cringe?

Oh, I speak as if we were old and married, friends of comforting non-desire, jokes and long-winded cigarettes. Perhaps I should have first mentioned sex.

A demain mon cher, dors bien,
Kati

PS I can bear conclusions no more than you,

Dear Alain,

But perhaps this will change when I bear children. The idea of
timelessness strikes me as an Einstein truth, don't bother me
Edith except on Wednesday at these hours. Being/Event/Subject
whatever, the child is crying and if I don't clock it will be too late.
I'm interested in a cosmology where birth is the center. Smile.
I wonder if you are like the other New York intellectuals: you
secretly despise feminists because you like it soft and wet and
dripping and often. I like it that way too, but it seems there is
some logic to the companionship process which eludes me. A
friend said there must be a historical justification for my myriad
short-term lovers, but that's just poetic exoticism, as recently
defined in the DSM V. Either way I admire Manon Lescaut for her
wiles. Funny, I can write a love letter to a philosopher, but I'm
just as hapless as those broads on Jerry Springer when it comes
to "commitment". I supposed it's been a timing thing, blame the
stars. Venus in Scorpio. Maybe you'll read this letter.

Yours,
K

Dear Alain,

I whisper things to you all day long. At midnight I try to put it into song. Everything I think to say seems inadequate, so I will tell you everything. Pulling memories of lines for you I can see why the love letter is out of style. Gil Scott Heron said, "Fuck a job and money / because I spend it all on unlined paper / and I can't get past / dear baby." Dear Alain.

Yours, Katy

Dear Alain,

The words, Alain. The language around me sticks like glitter. Did you ever see a middle class, American white girl in the 90s? She used that glitter make-up once and it stuck for decades. Now we have Lady Gaga.

Mostly to be less lonely I cling to the myths here around me. Like Lady Gaga. To say anything other than "people enjoy her and dance" would be too violent and historical to be true. But honestly? She makes me outraged with that lyric "you and me could write a bad romance." The whole country listens to this stuff. No wonder the best congressional orator is sarcastic Steven Colbert. No wonder we're crazy.

Dear Alain,

You take me out of the intimate, out of the tribal, away from myself to a communion with the farthest souls. For to speak of a truth is not to speak at all of you or me or us, but of all of us, most importantly the ugliest. I preach too much. Only I wish to say that reading you puts me in a glass case of looking, where I am small against it all. I think it's called alienation.

For you, I'll forgo all the details. Like the hot rollers, deep red nail polish, four collared coat and bourbon cocktails on a first winter's eve in crisp air tasting anxiously of snow. It's cold here, and I feel the time pass, restlessly, though events seem to be passing right under my nose. Barack Obama is less than a mile away, but we all feel so helplessly disinterested. My coat is a much prettier subject of affection, like my loose curls and rouge talons.

X, k

Dear Alain,

It's still unclear what happened during that year of my life. Or later, two years after. Or now, the past five. Finding a vocabulary to put it all together...that's a courage I've barely time for, in an age when the personal narrative is pointillist, at best.

$E^{-2i\pi}=1$? I think if there is the square root of negative one, my divagations into the realm of intuition must be meaningful. Sometimes I know things without saying them.

Tonight, for example? You'd like it sunny side up.

Dear Diary?

Can he even see me if I don't believe in thought? If I don't believe in making sense? All that I've written, can he even hear?

Whatever. Lollipops.

Argh! Stop with the set theory baby I want to know the difference between how you love me and how you love your wife versus how you love a random peasant in Bolivia versus how you love Humanity. Is that a homomorphism? I want to know how it feels. I want to know what you would do for me that wouldn't do for peasant X. Is each letter to me, each of your thoughts a drop of love in my lap? But how many times do you write Slavoj each day? I want more. You keep coming. That's not mercy; it's arousal. What is IT? Tell me something about the indiscernible.

Dear Alain,

It's difficult to get through dinner saying only "true" things. Imagine a conversation where sarcasm and other inefficient superfluities are illuminated. And if the cannon is the bar? Only geniuses would speak. Therefore, one must endure and enjoy stupidity. Fini.

PS Fuck philosopher kings!

Corrollary? Even philosophers much have jokes and flaws and unnecessary comments.

Note: Love your flaws Alain.

Dear A,

Normally I wait for the wind to blow to write, but here we are
generating on the clock. Its part magic carpool ride and part
practicing balancing a dime. I've been thinking on your poles
of philosophy and mallarme. When you speak of this symbolist
and proto L=A=N=G=U=A=G=E poet as a pole, I hear several
principals – the pieces of the words which make us, the rhythms
that sustain us, the symmetry we strive for, and that magic
potion emotion which eludes our control, makes us human, if
you'll kindly accept my definition. I've heard it said that the only
truth is that we are completely hollow and seeing this idea to
completion leads one either to philosophy, poetry or the convent.
You praise the poet's solemn, lonely stature. In a paraphrase "it
cries to no one. It is alone. Shares with who will come. Like a
stirring wheat field."

Dear Alain,

I wanted to take a walk, see something new, find something to quench the thirst in my mouth. It wasn't a taste so much as a texture I was looking for. I settled on sweet sour pickles. Don't be jealous, I'm not pregnant.

I'd been so busy dancing with the mash. Sigh, socializing. If you wear make-up too long you forget what your face looks like. I wanted to let go of everything, and by that I mean pull my energy back into myself, a familiar memory of life where there is nothing to remember except my own selfish narrative seen as a little girl laughing at adult stupidity, knees to her chest on the front steps.

I wanted out of the immediate moment, wanted the cold air of remembering it won't always be this way, that I'm in love with time before I'm in love with anything else. I wanted to see, think like a parent, looking down with wise eyes.

There is this other state where time is a temper tantrum, a cloud of ants burrowing in my shoulders, anxiety organizing my forces before the computer screen. Automated directives, if you will. Makes me crabby and bossy, pretending to be in control. I guess all we really own is what we tell ourselves, but I still pay my bills and discuss the price of rent.

I wonder if you still have personal philosophies or if you've put them all in some professional form. I wonder if you take mine with tea and a bit of sugar, and if you mind leaves the axiom-checker on hold for a charmed moment. When I was little I dreamed of a boy who would love my ideas. I guess you just dreamed of ideas, if you dream at all. In a way it's more fitting for you not to dream, for you are structure, and I am the undefined, reminding the metal to melt sometimes. Thank you for reminding me to think. Beyond the sense. Cause besides you, my evening was cold, sweet, bread and butter chips. Fresh from the refrigerator. Slightly red pepper. Crisp. Juice. Smooth, well, slightly ribbed.

Love, K

Dear Alain,

It's cold here. Snowing all day. Cinnamon sticks and cider sounds good to me. What I mean to say is your tender hyper sensitivity, candle in the bathroom, racing words during indecision, calm stubborn, your glaring intransigence, brazen unadorned touch, my noah's flood as only with you, the played wet between us, is is

Soon.

Dear Alain,

My sexuality has always seemed more isolating to me than
anything. And when it does awake it terrifies me. One day it's
going to kill someone. It's nearly killed me. Soon I'll be old and
grateful to relax into warm conversations whose intent I have
less to question. Am I prudish? I'm open to suggestions. Perhaps
a looser sentence would be fitting? Perhaps more words would
alleviate the magnets?

Dear Alain,

Oh dear. Do you want to use dick and cock and pussy and wet
and tree trunk and all that uhg. Uhg. But, darling, that's evil,
naming the unnamable. My brain went blank and collapsed in a
kaleidoscope. remember nothing, cubes, no words, etch. a. sketch.
the source, joy, break it again, break me any time, break me any,
any time, darling. But if you must. Juat not those words. They're
a prison from the real thing, an aesthetic profanity and, dear, you
know how serious I am about the source.

Yours,

Alain,

Oh my god you dirty motherfucker. I was serious! God don't go
there; I like it unnamable! Tell me what colors you saw or at least
more interesting words. It's not the dirt, I like it from behind, I
love when you exhasp over my silhouette but damn! the structure
of those words! the point is to dissolve –

Boo.
Lv, k

So where's *your* body, Alain?

Subsume your emotions into your dick. Fuck it out, go ahead.
Good baby.

As for your ideas about the female position, I'm not even gunna
go there. But I like that you are (nothing) in this book.

Not pretend or wall or I get something but I see you naked all your stupid problems and all I want is your stupid eros on my agape and my stupid thanatos and our stupid eros streaming in the concept of knowing each other. And steaming after the period. Then.

I just wanted to see you shake. Because it broke my heart and it was better than anything that way virgin everything that way some bullshit langauge about found something of finding prepositions in a text book you skin had goose bumps your hair on edge and you swallow help up on my perfection and I wanted nothing but to be perfect for you. No literary period. Naked breathe waiting hard terse waiting hard for permission into soft for more than permission for need for better than need for natural. For love.

And then oh it was cold unpoetic. Sigh. Exhaust. But it was. And it was an engaging for this chais was just as good being insulted to my face because my jacket didn't fit your tribe and I loved it the tribalism not because its utopian because its ideal and we huddled in our neuroses they kept us warm they huddled everywhere most of all where I knew you and loved you we were warm. That's an idea that keeps my warm. All of us naked goosebumps hard cock wet pussy with the skin smooth.

There and then and it happened and it was totally cliché like the catholics said and I didn't care clascritution fuck them I'm going to have my making blue all mine cubism music digital pointillism pick your favorite adjective here literally. That's it. Pick I'm picking hallelujuah spelled wrong in another language who gives a hot a guck given here not a panting I don't negatives the surface the who cares it was you it was you shimmering and I'll only ever see your shimmer but is it too poetic to say you came on solid substance wet and it meant nothing it meant nothing it meant nothing. And I thought those thoughts again and I thought it meant everything. Or the grapefruit and I'll go on meaning oh well. I love you that's it cliché whatever forever. That's it.

And you shook like. I wrote it. in the botes they said something about concepts whatever all. I. could. Think. But was your jelly

sentence out no periods I put them literarily like you anxiety
from the ___ but frat boy for crotch in a beautiful way

Dear Alain,

Naw. I just deconstructed my narrative again.

But you can help me put it back together? I can be Yoshi. You can be princess.

And boo, I'm sending you this book in the mail. *Tender Buttons*. You've read it, right?

x

"Keep Going! Continue to be this some-one, a human animal among others, which nevertheless finds itself seized and displaced by the eventual process of a truth." – A.B.

$$k_{n+2} + \alpha_{n+2}$$

"The point of being of the nothing
[the] multiple inconsistent whose dream is induced
by the non-being of the one." – A.B.

Dear Alain,

Oh so it turns you on to see my death drive? Is this some kind of objectification?

You do realize in my terms this is merely an episode of bad Pluto placement – but I digress. What I mean to discuss is the aspects of your venus –

Lap that up,

Dear Alain,

Mercury went retrograde Dec 10th, and does not go direct until Dec 30th and I would like to submit my letters to you towards evidence in the chart of modern astrology. Also, I read Endymion to my friend Megan in the drive from Washington to Cleveland. It was a delightful way to spend an early Christmas Eve! Do you celebrate Christmas? I wonder if these traditions are too conventional for you. There was a time when I would be angry that Christmas is not Christ's birthday but a convenient way for the Christians to eclipse the pagan's winter solstice. It's all political bullshit! And there's always the atheist in me horrified by blind faith, blah blah. These days I figure everyone has faith in something, from philosophy to something more mundane, like electricity. Convention is just as arbitrary as deconstruction, and it pisses my mother off less. (I think we've talked about this already.) Bottom line, I wonder who you spent your holiday with, and if you thought of me.

I won't bemoan it if you did not. I've plenty of daydreaming to do. And there's always facebook to entertain me and ease the loneliness. You won't be the first or last to ignore my advances anyway. One deconstruction I won't let go of, my feminism. I do love the chase.

Since my love for you is so clearly unrequited, I've been thinking, what is the difference between these letters and a public journal like facebook? I wonder if constant social networking is at all effective for making more healthy, relieved human beings. In a psychoanalytic, say-it-get-over-it, kinda way. It seems to be working for the politicians, like a new soma, though it's hard to measure those things.

Do you have time to daydream anymore, Alain? Will you ever retire? Perhaps this is the difference between the poet and the philosopher: you work for years on the next pencil mark of the same blueprint. Sometimes different rooms in different houses, but it's all one building. Poets, roughly speaking, we're sliding around in mud, rubbing it all over our faces, coating the grass with it, clapping our hands and laughing when a little bit of mud flies in the air. Smiling when the rain comes to wash us clean, hating the sun when it dries us to cracking. Like I said, we're at the origin, playing with words like playdoh.

I could have said "playing with words like clay" but I said "playdoh". See the traditional word would be clay but it's my job to use another word, because that clay image has been used before and so it's old or more precisely boring or ineffective. I guess the mature poet knows when to use the same old words for comforting images but in this career the Daoist approach is better when you're already established. See T.S. Eliot. Back to playdoh, there is another argument that says that word playdoh is too American a word, because it is an American brand. Also, it's exclusive to the group of people who can afford and are familiar with playdoh, so it is perhaps shallow. If a poet is going for universal, this word would be a no-no. Maybe aiming for universalism is akin to rooting for a bland, multi-national view of the world. But I think it would be beautiful if there was some poem that made most everyone smile. There's a principle there, besides ambition, but I bet you like it, you and your universal being subject event generic theory. It is an extra challenge picking words if one considers politics or social markers or audience. And then of course, how to stay fresh without only talking about nature images or something, ahem, universal. Especially because you turn this argument around and me writing you letters, you Alain Badiou, exclusive and unknown philosopher who loves the proletariat but speaks to an elite audience... Well now, I wouldn't be a poet if I did not love this contradiction. Good thing you have me because I bet you hate that contradiction. It probably makes you sad, or angry at the state of society, and moreover, it's your job to pull apart knots into straight pieces of rope.

Hang me. In a love can be fatal kind of way –

Merry Christmas,
Katy

P.S. Can you tell? I've got my period. All the sentences! Fitting somehow for a Christmas letter.

Dear Alain,

"Love what you will never believe twice"

Yes! Elsewhere fits quite nicely there...it could work...

you really do believe in the slow build and the denouement.

Dear Alain,

Oh I've been thinking like you so long I've turned into an old white man with a French cadence. It's sweet.

The paper this morning. "Desperate Global Hunt for Yield." Housing bubbles, gentrification. I never thought they could ruin bubbles for me but I can barely take a bath I hate that word and investors abstractly in a 19th century way. The rhyme is ruining even my child delight at spherical clear prisms. Air bubbles. And thought bubbles for it occurs to me that the worst gentrification is now happening in the hippest "ethnic" hoods. What was meant to discuss cultural acceptance became the tyranny of style... so much for human rights. I'm up with the situation and mine is implicated, but here we meant to set a trend of inclusion and the capital followed in intrusion, collusion, subterfusion, forced submission to a thought, many of them combining in a bubble – pop – over the actual situation. One example:

How's your coffee?

Dear Alain,

How can you stand me? I think through the stars – ancient – and energies – future – and I take faiths unproven, speculative judgmental and feeble. I crave them universal but they are new age or underage or anti-age or rediculage or outrage or anything but contemporary acclaim acceptable. Your Capricorn – oof - and my conspiring mind conspiring to go beyond go farther then we dare to Western now or then and both combined is what I try for now and who knows what it will be then - for I reserve the right to always change on a drop of mercury. You are the beautiful, all your thoughts a slow chiseled statue for consumption and mine clouds in the sky for dissolution or a momentary bloom of verse. And when they are dark or serious STOP, it shan't rain all day, it shan't be weight forever. HOPE.

If a single word could shatter a prison.

Every poets dream. Is it love? I know it's boring but it's true because thought blah whatever my heart doesn't give a damn what the fuck we think. It wants to know how you brush your teeth and what kind of toothbrush do you use and what are you wearing a shirt? Plaid flannel tie-waist pantaloons? How far from the ground? Mid calf because you are too tall? Do the creases in your knuckles stay after you've left the brush on the counter and for minute or three? Can I brush your hair off of your forehead and would you mind? Does your skin damp late in the evenings? And would you like for me to notice? Love a catalogue of preferences and kneeling giggling hallelujah before it. Something not thought at all, better than segmentation, a thing that melts the thoughts of your beloved makes them like crayon soft and insoluble to feed and clothe and satiate and tease and infuriate kindly and play and sandbox and blindfold and sigh and breathe + wonder + stop + pulse + calm + agony + small small agony the lovely kind and come and come again. And again. Utterance. Guttural. Nasal. No pattern.

You're always using this word finitude and I'm always using this word source. You call it a condition; I call it a Condition but who cares what it is, it is. It's as always and infinite and prescribed as math – cupid putti angel puck. Your language universal, But I'm talking about the post-proof universal solvent. Dissolve my everything, take me to winter's pace. Tell me you need to know about the cuticle on my toenail and the finest hair on my cheek. To think everything absurd or all as beautiful as smile. Cause it is and it melts from the thing aching to melt beyond you or me as other as matheme the thing we've always had and are always redefining pure as math

Dear Alain,

Fine, in your words.

Yours.

The real characteristic of the poetic event and the truth procedure that it sets off is that a poetic event fixes the errancy and assigns a measure to the superpower of the intellect. It fixes the power of the intellect. Consequently, the poetic event interrupts the subjective errancy of the power of the intellect. It configures the state of the situation. It gives it a figure; it configures its power; it measures it.

Empirically, this means that whenever there is a genuinely poetic event, the Intellect reveals itself. It reveals its excess of power, its repressive dimension. But it also reveals a measure for this usually invisible excess. For it is essential to the normal functioning of the intellect that it's power remains measureless, errant, unassignable. The poetic event puts an end to all this by assigning a viable measure to the excessive power of the intellect.

Poetry put the Intellect at a distance, in the distance of its measure. The resignation that characterizes a time without poetry feeds on the fact that the Intellect is not at a distance, because the measure of its power is errant. People are held hostage by its unassignable errancy. Poetry is the interruption of this errancy. It exhibits a measure for intellectual power. This is the sense in which poetry is "freedom". The Intellect is in fact the measureless enslavement of the parts of the situation, an enslavement whose secret is precisely the errancy of the intellect, its absence of measure. Freedom here consists in putting the intellect at a distance through the collective establishment of a measure for its excess. And if the excess is measured, it is because the collective can measure up to it.

We will call it a poetic prescription for the post-eventual establishment of a fixed measure for the power of the intellect.

Oh baby your language is driving me crazy. Not in a good way.
I like to melt and I'm totally on edge of melting in to boring
explanatory you, ooo.

Dear Alain,

I know nothing of being, except that I be here to love.

Oh, totally cute statement which evades the truth. I mean, it hurts to think so deep into the truth it makes my words boring! Uhg! Ok stop, I'm trying not to remember your terms so I can write today. But what I wanted to tell you was my memory of first wanting to meeting you. I never told you...

It was multiplicity inconsistent. Freedom from the oneness. These words are not my own: Mother, Doctor, Father, Neighbor, Grandma, Auntie, Uncle, Neighbor, brother, babysitter, etc. When you are about to call I feel your voice. I think "Alain", as if I can hear you thinking, "I haven't called her today." And then you call. I read too much of you. My poems come out coated with your words, in your rankings, your rhythms, your pragmatic concisions. We think of it differently, I think, but I am not myself, but the collection of all I have ever known or touched. Like Juliana says, we breathe the same air, every being on earth. I hope you don't mind my poetic interpretation. But I agree: One is a useless entity.

I think of it this way: each of us the singular infinite combination of our impressions, our experiences, our loves, our brushes with the universe.

Lv, k

Dear Alain,

Uhhhg. Yes Ok. Alright. Let's get technical. Ok. So. Pure being is
infinity. Or multiple possible infinities because there are infinite
infinities. Great. But in short, pure being is infinity because it can
go in any possible direction. The person, or individual, is singular.
So I guess what I wanted to say, strictly, about the individual was
that they are singular but influenced and created by an infinity of
factors, and connections, webs, links, liens, words, breathes and
moments to the infinity of other beings they have ever met or
read or seen on TV or encountered. You dig? Ok, so, in short, we
are singular multiplicities. That is our "being". And Pure being,
obviously, is like as multi-dimensional infinite insanity as the
Star Trek universe. As for Pure Being = math; sure, whatever you
want. I mean, the only thing I can say is that when I read Derrida
he always made me have an existential crisis, but when I did
math, I could do it for 12 hours straight and come up happy as a
clam. Very meditative actually. I think it's very true that math as
we know it is pure thought; non-judgmental so to speak, just the
purest lines in the sky. Yes, did I see that moment where I could
think without words? Absolutely. Think in images, in lines, in
pictures in space. Being-Qua-Being? Of course. And as a poet, it's
my job to stay in that space. All the time. Pretty great, huh? Are
you jealous? Jk. Ok I don't know if you agree with me that poetry
is in that space, but I can tell you, that *my* poetry is from that
space. That knowing beyond language. The great mathematicians
say: the difference between a numbers cruncher and the pure
mathematician? Intuition. And well, if you know the way to keep
that space from descending to the void? Please do tell me. So far,
I've only consulted Carl Jung and everyone else I know. Are they
connected? I think the void, for me, is what I saw when I was
forced by politics to be completely rational. I never want to ever
be there again. Because all I could see was the hopeless.

Love,
k

Ms. Bohinc,

You always have to be on top.

Yours, Alain

Alain,

I will be the bottom the wall the washing machine

Aries.

*

Hehe. I like horoscopes. You know what's nice about them?
They're equivalent. I mean, I've seen bad horoscopes, but I mean
everyone has one. If you assume all cultures are equal lens, like
India, China, Sudan, France, Ancient Greece, wherever, then I
thought I would try horoscopes for a while, to take a trip and
learn a new set of cultural mores, social standings, rules and
regulations, if you will. Anything to get out of America. Uhg.
America is like that guy at the bar who is in his mid 30s or 40s
and hasn't dated any one in while, just fucked for the past five
years, and has started to see things as a) alpha, b) beta, c) gamma
all based on hot, medium, ugly – "but you, you're different" –
UHG! I could kill him with a kitchen knife! That's capitalism,
always surface ranking. But horoscopes, what a pleasant divide.
The busboy could have the sweetest chart you ever saw. The
president a mass of jungle fucked oppositions. There are always
eight planets and twelve houses at play. So instead of boring
labels - "middle aged, loveless douchebag" or "beautiful young
thing" or "rich" or "poor" or dominant American culture "high,
low, forgettable" – SO BORING - instead I read a chart and get this
complex system of complex adjectives which beyond alleviating
my thirst for complexity also seems leveling. Each chart has a
complex personality. You know, like a human being. Of course
"hierarchical aspects" remain – the tenth house is fame or
ambition or social standing, for example. But it's always paired
with other considerations like water, air, fire or earth personality,
dreamer, pragmatist, energetic or staid. And where the mind sits
versus where the heart sits, versus where the energy sits, versus
where the Neptune, Uranus, Pluto or Saturn sits. Oh yum. Plus
then I can pretend I'm living in the middle Ages, or Greece or
Early Syria or the Fertile Crescent. You know medicine was based
on astrology until the Middle Ages! Like for a stomach ache on
the left side that's the liver which is ruled by Taurus so take these
pills on Tuesday – the Taurus day – at 2 AM when the moon is
strong and at quarter strength. It would make me irate today, but
everything makes one irate or is causing cancer anyway, what's
the difference if it's from the Middle Ages. Luckily the Middle
Ages, seem so far off that I only vaguely imagine the hard labor,
mud, lack of toilet paper, short quick fucks in the sidestall on rank

breath and stinking boots. All my images from Hollywood. But I would like to really go there. Should I re-read Beowulf? I want to see the sparks flying off the knives as they sharpen in the street the metal workers and a big grand un female fire. Not the social dynamics. The soot and the ledger.

Oh dear you should like them too, horoscopes, come to think of it. They are a lot like set theory. Or the multiplicity of sets. And each soul's singularity.

Dear, let's not be star crossed lovers

"Is thought obliged to endure Thermidorean frameworks of its own Ruination?" – A.B.

$$k_{n-1} + \alpha_{n-1}$$

"Evil...is to want, at all costs and under condition of a truth, to force the naming of the unnamable" – A.B .

Cultural revolution and killing fields and the holocaust that's what is it to kill by category but to kill for thought and this is wrong because it breaks hearts and only love doesn't make the mistake of thought and death by it because love is blind as surely my shoulders are blind to anything but loss over these thoughts I've come up against these thoughts...

It is not violence. It is not violence. I saw the best of my generation raving hysterical naked it is not violence the best of my generation raving hysterical naked it is not violence it is not violence it is not violence I saw the best of my generation raving hysterical naked how do you think they got that way it is not violence it is not violence I saw them shot I saw the boy forced to shoot his brother I saw the wife and the child shot, axed, tortured, burned, slain, slaughtered, raving hysterical naked I will commit no violence if I live to do one thing I will commit no violence I will leave no man raving hysterical naked I will heal I will leave no one in pain I will leave no man raving hysterical naked I will not be violent and when I die I will say one word I lived my life in justice and that is all no one near me broke before my knowledge without a handful of cups and bandaid fragment utterances the best I could do. And violence begins with the broken tone don't forget that words are violent too and I will be silent before I am violent to you, ever, you watch your words Monsieur Badiou, you watch your tone, you are, you are violent too, sometimes, offhand, you forget, you fill with yourself. No violence. No violence of the universal, no violence no raving hysterical naked nothing but the lyric I and ears. I understand but i disagree. No violence. Love is what bleeds through and swamps your philosophy. And pain too. but forget that forget it for. get. it. love love love before we forget that too love love love love love love love love love love love love love love love love did you ever meet someone who doesn't know what love is? IT is not violence. IT is love. Teach them love. Teach them all love. It's as impossible as anything good rising from the ashes of blood.

FUCK YOU.

BUT I SHOULD BE INTEGRAL AND THINK LIKE YOU.
LEAVE

CANT

Love is more than a thought. Love is more than what you think.
Love is more than ideology. Down with ISMS. DIDN'T YOU LEARN
ANYTHING FROM THE CULTURAL REVOLUTION?

I know what you think. I CANT BEAR IT. SHOULD I KILL YOU?

NOTHING CAME FROM THE CULTURAL REVOLUTION EXCEPT
THE MEMORY OF OUR THEORIES their drowned failures RAVAGE
RAVAGE RAVAGE ENEMY the END OF LOVE THE TORTURE OF
LOVE THE TORTURE OF THINKING TWO AS ONE TORTURE
OF THINKING TWO AS ONE they all thought TWO AS ONE they
thought TWO AS ONE AND TWO AS ONE AND WHAT DOES
EVERYONE AROUND ME THINK

BUT IT WAS PARANOIA IT WAS FEAR IT WAS DEATH IT WAS
FEAR IT WAS DEATH IT WAS TERRIBLE TOO TERRIBLE FOR
WORDS TO UTTER IT WAS THINKING AS OTHERS CONSTANTLY
CONSTANT OTHER CONSTANT OTHER CONSTANT OTHER SAY
THAT A MILLION TIMES BEFORE YOU SLEEP EACH NIGHT
CONSTANT OTHER CONSTANT OTHER CONSTANT OTHER

SAY THAT A MILLION TIMES BEFORE YOU SLEEP AT NIGHT
CONSTANT OTHER CONSTANT OTHER

ALL WORK AND NO PLAY MAKES JACK A DULL BOY
CONSTNANT OTHER CONSTNAT OTHER CONSTNT OTHER
THINK AGAIN, ALAIN. THINK AGAIN. Think again in terror. Not in
sadness not in fear not in tragedy in terror. In terror and sadness,
fear and tragedy every day every moment for six or seven or eight
or more years. Think again until you cannot think any more. Until
you cannot think of what another wishes except with fear. Or, "I
Hope" "Be Well" and that is all. That is as far as thought will take
you. Because after that thought there is too much pain to go on,

to do anything but go to bed or take account of the dishes or the ledger or anything as dry as dry as dry as anything that doesn't make you cry. Think again Alain. You have no idea.

The Cultural Revolution didn't break the bonds, it turned the bonds to kryptonite. Put a cigarette out on someone as you walk down the street. Watch a car explode and burn them alive. Don't stop. He's pissing you off, pop.

THINK AGAIN IN TERROR MAYBE YOU WILL UNDERSTAND. NOT IN SADNESS NOT IN FEAR NOT IN TRAGEDY IN TERROR.

*

YOUR HUMANITY FUNCTION IS BROKEN!!!

Dear Diary,

The skin is peeling off my back, from the nape of my neck through my shoulder blades. In bile I trust. I write to pronounce to flake the skin off these words to dry the wound. That was a real sentence. The sentences will be real until there is no longer a chance. I can still go back.

I can't believe he could think that. The pain of it will always ring in my ear each lecture from his throat. The dripping erotic that was the sound of home the sound of still water or rock or soft mellow and now it's just electric fucked because it's all a lie. To propagate that thought. The evil of it. He's such a fucking human being. Which would be fine except I just can't bear to hear him sort through my thoughts de-kinking them and kicking each one until it's his, limp, begging on the floor, and me sitting there knowing that if his blood ever dared run so warm to bleed into his brain he would collapse at the pain of it all. Oh his ideas his dreams. Can I bear it?

And what of me? Who am I to speak, I who say fuck the ideas, there is only the floating poem. That the sentences, even the math will all amount to nothing in the absolute cruelty of the mess of the human, and no amount of literature or Greek tragedy or attempts at anything will save us from ourselves. Or some of us might save ourselves, and some of us do try, but what of the rest, there's no hope for all the rest for so many of us, so many who already do not know love. Shall we slaughter the loveless? Kill those messy souls; eliminate them from our wretched plan. Like I eliminate Alain? Who am I to run away?

Oh he made a fancy rubric good for him. It's just a fucking fancy rubric. You always said love was greater than any architecture. The blood in the spreadsheet and here you are saying love isn't big enough to seep through this grand cross. No not big enough for this. Not big enough to seep through. Your body doesn't seem to care. Your heart doesn't give a damn it's radiating through you shoulder blades, shimmering scalding blue.

And isn't this precisely the lesson of the cultural revolution, the one we must never never never never learn again the one we must always remember and take everywhere and preach everywhere and never ever ever ever ever learn again, that thought is nothing thought is wretched, thought is nothing nothing nothing compared to the heart, compared to pain compared to the tragic the wretched wretched of wretched and there should be love above all above all else because only love can stop and be greater than the war of words or ideas or categories because it can seep through and it does seep through and our categories will never be big enough and if we kill by them if we decide by them we will always murder and delete and love is the only anecdote. There is no category in love.

Maybe that's the point; the categories are still there, still sensed. The loss, the pain is that you couldn't overcome with him. Couldn't seep into that nothing-everything. And now it's wretched.

Dear Alain,

I won't get mad. I won't. I'm fucking trying here. I won't give you
that pleasure. I won't call you mother fucker. I won't scream. I
won't "give you that part of me I won't give anyone else". What
you don't understand, is I am the genius of creating another
home. Another world where screaming doesn't exist. It's me, this
is what I am creating. You don't have to love me for it. It's not
even sweet. It's probably another form of terrible. But this is the
rubric you must confine to. This is where I stand.

I'm talking about love im talking about something that wakes me up and night and ravishes me for you and it's not it has nothing to do with thought I couldn't think my way into you I can't think my way out of you I can only think a million ways why everything is wrong but I still love you I still throb I still wake up and think of you think right think wrong I think only of you and that's not from any thought that's thought trying to keep up with the heart

I love you.
Me

You said poetry is fucking elsewhere so how can you see me if love is thinking for two and you fucking think I'm elsewhere? It's just a fucking paradox we can't work out if love is thinking as two. So it's not. And all the other things we disagree about. Or your definition of poetry is wrong. OR FUCKING SOMETHING IT'S NOT WORKING OUT IN FUCKING THEORY.

Dare I say it? You're all fucking wrong. The best of what we are: lovers stuffing mud in the inevitable fissures, cracks, splinters, fractions, irrationally repeating decimals, holes, gaping, schisms, shatters, frayings, frictions, failures, errors. I am not perfect. You are subordinate to art, philosophe. You are subordinate to history, to reality, to parables, to metaphor, to pain, to injustice, to inevitability, to tears and to life. There is no solution to this condition. There is morality. There is prayer. There is weeping kneeling god fuck me I am fucking sorry and grateful for my existence and I will try to make this wretched life so little better as I can. For you, for me, for everyone I touch.

Dear Alain,

This birthday is the first to make me say, "I hate birthdays." I have been feeling intensely the deep weight and frigid chill of ice in my veins – the creeping, raging sense of failure.

I have to deal with my life. I cannot do this with you in it. I thought I could. I would have loved to take up Philosophy and logic and Paris. Maybe start an orphanage in the banlieues when you retire. I've always dreamt of an orphanage.

But we are both too slow and too crazy. And too hard and too obsessive. I have to deal with my life now. Part of the sense of failure related to having chased you for so long. I know you do not believe me, but I do love you with an intensity I have never before experienced. When we make love, I cry, not because I am in pain, but because I am in love. Silly you has never seen this in a woman before?

You said your new project was honesty with Katy I wanted to slap you. But I am not surprised. I've always known you held deep relationships wherein the others bonded but you did not. This is a kind of lie I detest. Particularly in a man whose life is "truth". I will not regret the time I spent with you ever. I will only testify that there is a kind of desire that made me insane and forget all else, the kind of desire that has been written of for years and ages. I don't owe you any of this and I should not even be honest with you – you took my heart and held it dripping, licking the blood with the sweet language of your mind, but not your heart, and not your honesty. I do not respect you, but I will always love you. I was "not like the others" you were more, by many times, of any of the rest. Take this as truth. Take my insanity.

I've got to go write some poems.

Fine you wanna go there? You're just a tool. I have no respect for you. I hope they buy my book because a boring white man is involved.

I don't even remember how to be artful anymore; your desert is suffocating and your cultural revolution is ignorant mis-infinity anti-calculation on the scale of Rumsfeld. Dry out for this? Are you fucking kidding me? The sex isn't even good. You can't melt. I hope you're crying. I hope you cry and feel the abyss. You might know an ounce '68-'76, and maybe you have a fucking inkling of the terror your thought Thermidored into.

What YOU'VE GIVEN!?! MY LANGUAGE! You stupid fuck. I've grown boring and stupid and self dribble sitting around with your old man white ass. You don't understand anything except the professional lovely and the perfectly argued proof, please you infinity dries me up inside. And all this sacrifice for what, for you who think the cultural revolution is an interesting thought experiment? Uhg I want to vomit on your wrinkles. Everything is just a thought experiment to you, isn't it. I'm just a thought experiment to you! What's it like to be with a poet? Tell me? How is it? My heart, and a billion Chinese just a thought experiment to you? Murder, just a practice at breaking bonds? You're a piece of shit and the banality of that insult suits you.

STOP I cant fucking breath here I have to go.

FUCK YOU AND YOUR BREAKING BONDS ALL WE HAVE IS
BONDS THAT'S ALL WE FUCKING HAVE AND IF THAT MEANS I
CANT HAVE TRUTH THEN I DON'T. FUCKING. WANT. IT.

Look I went for the Joycean fucking departure and there's a
reason why *Ulysses* is all about Dublin. I went to the revolution
numbed my bonds to kelvin left them with language at the door
of progress and I am a fucking militant too. I fucking am. But it's
not what you say. It's that we can do better than what you say. We
can do it with love too.

Now stop, my fucking heart is breaking.

HOW CAN I BE IN THE MOMENT IF YOU WILL NOT GET THE FUCK OUT OF MY FACE?

DON'T WORRY DARLING, DEATH IS MERELY A WORLDLY PRINCIPAL OF STABILITY.

There was nothing interesting about it at all. Nothing. It didn't free people from bonds it destroyed the capacity to bond. You can still see it today there isn't a place like it on earth. Maybe Angola. You can't fucking think that Alain. Love is a condition on your politics.

You can't fucking write that. It's breaking my heart to write this. This truth.

Now stop. We can do better. We must.

So it is that the defeat of the ethic of a truth, at the undecidable point of a crisis, presents itself as a betrayal." – A.B.

$$k_{n-2} + \alpha_{n-2}$$

"Ultimately what true politics undermines is the illusion of the bond" – A.B.

And I understood your language, down to the scraped layer

of cake. If cake was as good as hearing your words all over

again and again an avant eruption of noise each frag reborn

Dear Alain,

I'm here in DC, before the White House. There are arguably 500 people here all in solidarity with Turkey. Terrific for the humid and generally humid brained Washington. And of course I can't stop crying. I don't even know these people and must look like a clown. I think it's OK for poets to cry. We must cry for all of us.

How many here have family in Turkey who faced a tear gas canister and walked away dripping chalky bleeding thoughtless spined-forever in a way it might our blessing not to be. I hope the Children lay always supine and silly. No need for needing to steel. That's not infinity. But how it begins. It doesn't matter. What matters but the large heart beating as one. To say it's wrong and it to be true by no other measure than the heart rising up from pain not down from platitude but up from that well spring "enough" up

That human thing that says "human" and under which we are all truly equal and which view we should always fight for in everything. That moment when social critique is a detail too fine to grasp or see and matter under the haunting reality of HUMAN and somehow nothing brings that out like a crowd of strangers sweaty, tired, throbbing in the night against police and macho architecture.

Dear Alain,

a bff from college spent two years in turkey and now works at
the turkish embassy. she and i were always very different - she
always made fun of my Occupy tendencies. but she called me last
night to say "i cant go to the DC solidarity march (for political
reasons since she works at the embassy); can you go for me?" we
both cried. "who would have imagined, me?" she said.

It is far from over, far from over.

I can hear the protest outside my window as we speak. It's
obvious that it will be Tiananmen Square or Erdogan will resign.
I wonder if it will spread to Europe next. A world then, of the
Greeks, of Abraham, in smolders of the people trying again
against two poles of Chinese American dictatorship? I can hear
the conservatives now: power of the people led to rubble, thus...

It is far from over, far from over. A Drake song in my head. The
next line "what am I doing? What am I doing? Oh, that's right,
that's right, I'm doing me, I'm doing me." I'm not sure if doing me
is the realization of the truth process or the fall of civilization but
it is happening. And I weep. Oh it's so god damned beautiful. And
they say Egypt is a mess; it will be a hell for Turkey, but France
had quite a few republics before it got cool. I still believe. I'll take
a rubble sorting through truth over a manufactured consent any
day. And that's where I stand; and that's my truth and I'm sticking
to it I don't give a damn what anyone says I know because I cry
when we stand I know in my heart that's it's not anarchy it's not
ignorant although it is those things it's truth from the bottom of
the heart the only thing that makes us different from computers
the only thing that makes philosophy legitimate it's otherwise
fucked in this sense nature does not exist I get it but you're
still nuts and I still love you even though I hate you just for the
one thing you say about believing in infinity in that moment of
standing up that moment right now in Ankara in Istanbul in Gezi.
Maybe the poet and the philosopher come together in revolution.
Maybe this *is* infinity. Maybe I'm watching it right now on TV.
Where the point is a line and the line is a circle and the circle
a flower where the vortex inverts and SOMETHING HAPPENS.

What are you doing to me, Alain? What are you doing, what are
we doing? Why can't I stop writing you, why can't I stop loving
you, why? But we're here and I stand and I call it love. We can
have it too. We already do. In this moment we make love and
it is real and tomorrow it will break you too much logic and
symmetry and me all poetry but for this moment we are and it's
infinite and I will stand to say it's true and isn't that all you ever
asked? So isn't this all it is? Am I the woman? Am I the man? You
need to shove your fixed positions down your thick throat with
your tall man hands but right now it doesn't matter we agree on
this, we are alive at dawn on the horizon and the future will bring
us back to reality only if we let it. I need your heart with me this
time. I need it back together. Tell me. Tell me. Tell me. I love you.

Dear Alain,

And I think the only world view worth having is the spinning
fragmented madness of the hangover. The swirling heaving
breathing panic attack which sees the world and cultures as crass
mass judgments and nasty cultural characteristics like people
running mad all over the word making chaos and every once
and a while a huge nasty orgasm erupts like in Turkey crying for
some god damn alignment for what is good. And you nothing you
wretched architecture. You are nothing. And I am not fucking you
right now Alain. You're nothing but a dead object to me. The most
human breathing thing you do is to make those awful mistakes
and then I see and I hate you or something colder and but at
least that, that is a feeling. You don't open me up to the insane
whirlwinds of life, you put them in a box, and I cant see them
there and I must leave. The poet is not in the philosophy and I am
going I am going I am gone. Democracy. Me.

Dear Alain,

Dear God won't you just go to hell already, get out of my mind, out
of my metaphors. I speak, I say, that's what Badiou says. I think,
I hear your lines tinkling in the view. I am surrounded by your
lines, lines, lines, lines, lines, and all I want is jazz and all I hear is
Badiou, and all I want is spicer's cable cars and lang's swamp, the
rustled folds of coan silk, a poem without a single bird in it, 22nd
century, blues and roots, the rustled folds of coan silk. Damn. Get
out, you lines. Get outta here. I feel your tattoo, badiou. I feel your
tattoo. But only in my brain. It's gray. And charred.

Dear Alain,

I went to sleep in the soft folds of ego submitted to the logic
of nothingness and it felt so much better than you. If that was
a thing I would say if that were true. If that were true all I
would say is I forget everything but the point on the pointillism
and your hands in my hair and there would be nothing but a
harmonic hum there would be no word better there would be no
thought whatsoever. You. You. Dear Badiou.

Dear Alain,

Love is the kind of thing that pulls the rubix cube to pieces. You are the kind of thing that puts the rubix cube to parts.

"There will always have been a challenge laid down by art to the concept, and it is on the basis of this challenge, this wound, that it is necessary to interpret the Platonic gesture which can only establish the royalty of the philosopher by banishing the poets." – A.B.

$$k_n + \alpha_n$$

"the beginning"

"[Love has] an imperative function: continuing always, even in separation, and which holds that absence is itself a mode of continuation." – A.B.

Dear Alain,

When everything went mad. I didn't think of you. When the boy with the sweetest heart got the prize his parents never gave him and his world was healed those cracks in the struggle and the sarcasm melted with love everything went mad and I didn't think of you, not once. I thought of Rumi, Stephen, Doug, Meg, Brandon, Anne, CA, Ryan, Bernadette, beauty, love, Maged, Buck, Brilliance, my mother, tears, joy and silence. But you were elsewhere. Lyric. I thought of all the pauses and the tones and eye glances when everything went mad.

When everything goes mad, I hope you're well.

Love always,
Your Katy

However you remember

Dear Diary,

Only years later did I realize: I wanted to be on the bottom.

MATH POLITICS LOVE

PHIL ⟷ POETRY

Malcolm X Park, Washington DC

C. Paul Jennewein's Armillary Sphere
A winged baby, Putto, stood in the center
Of this fully functioning nearly 6 foot tall astrolabe
Donated by Bertha Noyes 1936
Mysteriously disappeared late 1970s

This strange book, *Dear Alain*, by Katy Bohinc can be represented as such: you have a great countryside named "Alain Badiou," the park of Alain Badiou. And she looks and walks through the park, with a perspective supported by a thought, an effect, maybe even, a love? This book is the collection of thoughts of Katy Bohinc, who – armed with a reader's eye and surrounded by profound effects – retains, sorts, and rejects the different aspects of the park she visits. She knows there exists under the name "Alain Badiou," a park, and so she addresses him, this supposedly dear Alain, at times with affection, at times in anger, at times almost indifferent, and at times revealing forcefully her difference and opposition through the poetic vehemence of her writing to the serenity she sees in the park of philosophy. Day after day, Katy returns to this park and her eye changes, her relationship with "Alain Badiou" varies like the time that passes, and her thoughts inscribe themselves in small texts that in the end compose a kind of ode to the park.

Like there is an ode to the Greek urn or an ode to a champion of the Olympic Games, there is an ode in the prose-poem of Katy Bohinc to the park of Alain Badiou. She is the fierce and lucid visitor of a good number of corners of this park. She knows also that she hasn't seen everything; she cannot see everything. But she desires to, one day. Having put in her poetic writing all the park of philosophy, she notes that only with two simultaneous writings can it be true love, and such is the dream to which the beautiful book *Dear Alain* testifies, fragmentarily, but forever.

Alain Badiou, June 24, 2014, 4 PM, Paris.

Translation, katy bohinc

Compatibility:
With Birth Times

katy (poetry)
Cleveland, OH United States 11/19/1983 18:04
Julian day 2445658.46
Adjust 5.00 ST 21.31 Lat 41.30 Long 81.41

Alain (Philosophy)
Rabat Morocco 01/17/1937 12:00
Julian day 2428551.00
Adjust 0.00 ST 19.19 Lat 34.02 Long 6.51

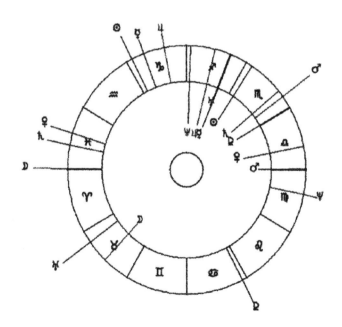

katy	Aspect	Alain	Orb/Value	
Sun	Sextile	Sun	0.0	472
Sun	Trine	Moon	0.24	304
Sun	Trine	Pluto	0.37	81
Moon	Trine	Mercury	0.58	169
Moon	Sextile	Saturn	1.24	69
Moon	Trine	Neptune	1.21	73
Venus	Square	Jupiter	0.40	-142
Mars	Trine	Sun	3.56	81
Jupiter	Square	Saturn	2.15	-77
Jupiter	Square	Neptune	2.18	-66
Saturn	Trine	Venus	3.15	52
Saturn	Conjunction	Mars	3.25	88
Saturn	Sextile	Jupiter	0.56	56
Saturn	Opposition	Uranus	3.59	-32
Neptune	Square	Moon	1.10	-117
Pluto	Square	Pluto	2.53	-42
		1445	-476	969

Inter-planetary aspects

The following aspects between planets concern the possible relationships between two charts: especially the emotional and romantic relationship, but also aspects on social, intellectual and spiritual levels.

katy Sextile Alain Sun - Sun

Positive aspect: It's an excellent aspect for a union because neither has to explain to the other about his or her life goals and overall personality. The two people complement each other in basic ways. Although every relationship has its struggles and conflicts, this aspect helps strengthen your relationship because there is an overall understanding and you support one another at the end of the day.

katy Trine Alain Sun - Moon

Positive aspect: This is likely to be a significant relationship. There is a strong feeling of belonging to one another, for better or for worse, that keeps the two together. It's an excellent aspect for a union: they are made to go well together, to understand, appreciate, love and complement each other.

katy Trine Alain Moon - Mercury

Positive aspect: Ideal aspect for a couple, as they will have lots of interests and projects in common, and they will understand each other well. There is a mental rapport that sometimes borders on the telepathic.

katy Square Alain Venus - Jupiter

Negative aspect: A life together that can be very challenging at times on an intellectual level. Intellectual misunderstandings, diametrically opposed tastes, different ideas.

katy Square Alain Moon - Neptune

Negative aspect: This union will be full of illusions and disappointments. They will find it difficult to understand each other. Unfaithfulness and lies are on the agenda.

katy Conjunction Alain Mars - Saturn

Positive aspect: A life together with few problems. Love tends to develop into friendship. In a broad sense, they understand each other and go well together. Their relationship can be a little routine at times, and there may be some self-consciousness with each other.

This is one indication that they will be faithful to one another.

katy Trine Alain Sun - Pluto

Positive aspect: It's love-at-first-sight, the great passion: they will be drawn to each other like two magnets, they will always have to see and touch each other. Very good sexual understanding, typically very passionate. It must be said that this type of relationship may not last forever, it may not develop into a quiet and tender love. If they part, it is close to impossible to stay friends because of the constant reminder of the passion that once existed. It's all or nothing with them. If they part, one will suffer when the passion of the other dies, it will be a very difficult time to live through. However, if they stay together, there is strength to gain from each other.

katy Trine Alain Sun - Mars

Positive aspect: Pure sexual attraction can unite the couple. They feel as if they have an ideal partner. They will be energetic, full of life and can undertake things together on a professional level or travel together on adventurous, unpredictable journeys. They respect each other's goals and drives, and don't stand in the way of their attempts to achieve their goals. Their body rhythms match well, and they share a basic physical bond that is hard to break. Energizing.

katy Square Alain Jupiter - Saturn

Negative aspect: Difficult relationship as a couple, the two being too different even to complement each other.

katy Trine Alain Moon - Neptune

Positive aspect: An almost magical bond will unite them. Perfect harmony. There is something MORE to this relationship. It inspires the imagination, and there is a magical feeling of acceptance. There is much devotion here, especially on the part of the Moon person. Spiritual tenderness and romantic warmth between them. Their relationship encourages imagination in both people. This stems from an underlying acceptance of each other, which translates into the feeling that they are free to express their spiritual, imaginative sides without fear in each other's presence. Unconditional love, which is very rare in romantic partnerships.

katy Sextile Alain Moon - Saturn

Positive aspect: They will lead their lives together, with the Moon bringing fantasy to Saturn, who is sometimes too austere but whose other qualities (which the Moon does not possess) are appreciated. Two people whose difference in character is made to complement each other.

katy Square Alain Jupiter - Neptune

Challenging aspect: They sometimes encourage impracticality in one another. They often feel let down with one another, usually because each wants very much to please the other, but it is hard to fulfill all the promises that are made to one another.

katy Sextile Alain Jupiter - Saturn

Positive/Supportive aspect: This is not a defining element of compatibility, but it is supportive. A favorable union, a joyful family life. Thanks to Saturn, this couple rarely enters any adventure lightly and instead tends to work out and think things through. Many plans may be made together.

katy Trine Alain Venus - Saturn

Positive aspect: This union could be favorable and lasting, if Venus is really looking for a mature person to be with. There can be a certain level of self-consciousness together that is always present, no matter how long they are together. There is a lot of loyalty between them, and a feeling of responsibility for one another.

katy Opposition Alain Saturn - Uranus

Negative aspect: Challenging in terms of perspectives. There can be distinct times when they argue about restrictions on freedom.

Notes:

"The level of presentation, which only designates that some sort of multiplicity is in the situation" – A.B.

Translation: "a fraction of the notable moments, darlings." – K.B.

$$k_0 + \alpha_0$$

P 16 Euclid's plane, So they just met. And the phrase would be "generic plane". But she doesn't know him yet: "If one category has to be designated as an emblem of my thought, it would be neither Cantor's pure multiple, nor Godel's constructible, nor the void, by which being is named, nor even the event, in which the supplement of what-is-not-being-qua-being originates. It would be the generic." *Being and Event*, 15.

P 19 The ***, "The poem makes the moment of the empty page in which the argument proceeds, proceeded, will proceed." *Infinite Thought*, 81.

P 20 Mallarme (Stephen), Badiou primarily references Mallarme as a representative "pole" of poetry throughout his long oeuvre. Stephen Mallarme was a terrific French poet (1842-1898) known for wonderful word play, experimentation with presentation on the page, and logic games. Famous line, "a role of the dice does not abolish chance" (*un coup de dés jamais n'abolira le hazard.*)

P 20 Poetry at the origin, "Naturally it would be pointless to set off in search of nothing. Yet it must be said that this is what poetry exhausts itself doing." *Being and Event*, 54.

P 23 Think of writing for the entire of existence, "Philosophy cannot renounce that its address is direct to everyone, in principle if not in fact." *Infinite Thought*, 38.

P 25 Our wretched infinite, This line originally read "our wretched nothingness" but per Badiou's placement of the void, the void is literally the null set, and being is infinite multiplicity, defined only by its "opposition" or "index" against the void. See meditations 1-6 of *Being and Event*.

P 25 *When tomorrow becomes yesterday*, These lines are from a song by Nina Simone, "22nd Century". If you Google the lines you will find the song. A poetic technique used in American Avant Garde poetries: leave a message to be Googled. A game if you will, but it represents the "user" or "reader's" dependence on or interactions with Google.

P 30 You'll spend eternity with the maggots, "I would like this book to be read, appreciated, staked out, and contested as much by the inheritors of the formal and experimental grandeur of the sciences or the law, as it is by the aesthetes of contemporary nihilism, the refined amateurs of literary deconstruction, the wild militants of a de-alienated world, and by those who are deliciously isolated by amorous constructions." *Being and Event*, preface XV.

P 31 Philosophy is all moral consequence, There is a distinction here between "Philosophy" and Badiou. Badiou actually is different in this sense, his philosophy is designed specifically to evade moralistic judgment by describing the *process* by which a truth is determined, not by defining the truth itself, which, per Badiou, is the role of each singular individual, to decide their truth.

P 37 Real Projective Plane, A famous mathematician: Carl Friedrich Gauss (1777-1855). Many called him the greatest mathematician since antiquity. His contributions are lengthy. Among them, a system called the Real Projective Plane. As the story goes, Gauss was walking down the shore, looking at the horizon. And he said to himself, they told me parallel lines don't meet. But they DO meet; they meet at the horizon. So Gauss created a system, like an X-Y plane, but on it one could graph not normal X-Y coordinates, but, literally, what happens at infinity. The results are incredibly beautiful. In the Real Projective Plane, a point is a line. A line is a circle. And a circle is a flower. And so on.

$$k_1 + \alpha_1$$

P 45 Politics and Metaphysics, First, a false appropriation of the text which is actually called *Metapolitics*. The quotations are also a poetically symbolic gesture. Actually, Alain never says this at all. He says the complete opposite. I will summarize in my words what he lays out in the last chapter ("Politics as Truth Procedure", 141-152): Political events necessarily invite repression from the state. In doing this they expose the power of the state, which is normally hidden. So in a sense, political events measure the power of the state. This subtraction, the political event and the subtraction of the exposed power of the state, leaves a space for true equality to reveal itself. So, the political event is that where the event – the exposed power of the state, approaches 1, or equality.

My reference is a subtle inversion: The state's power cannot be quantified (it is infinite), and so the political event cannot be quantified either (they are also infinite).

P 49 A big void, To truly address Alain, the supporting term would be "a big infinite". But we do at times refer to old usages. To the poet - void/infinite/nothingness - these distinctions are somewhat irrelevant to the sensory preceptors. What we are discussing is sensory, not theoretical. But I'll also say, the use of void here is actually pretty good use, vis-a-vis Alain's eyes – it is a use of the void to rank, to index or measure what exists. Alain defines the void as a point of reference (nothing) against which Being shows her measure. Similar to zero.

P 50 Juvenile stuck on the problem of naming, The chapter "Politics of Thought", in *Metapolitics* addresses this question quite well. To summarize, the problem of naming exists, in that the act of naming limits in its inscription the set of information it contains. Per Badiou this difficulty is overcome by understanding that thought itself is an active entity, an incomplete site which describes not only what has been, but also what may be: "what happens does not cancel out the fact that what could have taken place lies behind the organization of the prescriptive statements." Alain discusses naming with regards to politics here, but we'll extrapolate towards naming and thought generally.

P 50 Your systems don't give a damn for psyche, "Psyche" is used here in reference to the psyche of poetry, which is an extremely complex term that refers to many things within the poetry community but I'll shortly translate it as the combination of sound, rhythm and lyric effect within a poem which denotes not only thought but an emotional or spiritual state.

P 50 Chinese woman who has never used a personal pronoun, *The Good Women of China*, Xin Ran. See chapter 15, "The Women of Shouting Hill". You will learn something about anthropology. As per representing Badiou, "Language is not the absolute horizon of thought. The great linguistic turn of philosophy, or the absorption of philosophy into the mediation of language must be reversed." *Infinite Thought*, 37. Agreed. Emphatically.

P 50 Events of Robespierre, "It is through St Just and Robespierre that you enter into this singular truth unleashed by the French Revolution, and on the basis of which you form a knowledge, and not through Kant or Francois Furet." I MUST add in this note, that this description suits me SOLELY to represent the truthful eyes of the militant as opposed to the power of the philosopher. Further,

it is imperative I add that I believe the militant title and exception extends through the stage of personal emancipation & activism and ENDS at the point of organized power. The distinction of power is obviously treacherously fine and problematic.
The feather pivot I do not know.

P 53 Ni hui ying yu ma?, (Mandarin for "Do you speak English?") "Philosophy privileges no language, not even the one it is written in." *Infinite Thought*, 38.

P 55 Mallarme thinks nothing but is pure form, This is obviously not a completely true or rational statement. She's just mad. Mallarme did things with form and he also wrote a lot of essays. He thought a lot. The description of Mallarme is a sort of proxy for the American L=A=N=G=U=A=G=E poetry, and the discussion here is certainly only one valence, far from final. We do say things when mad.

P 60 It's rather unnamable, I'll refer back to what is possibly my favorite line of Badiou's: "naturally it would be pointless to set off in search of nothing. Yet it must be said that this is what poetry exhausts itself doing." *Being and Event*, 54. "The unnamable is the point where the situation in its most intimate is being submitted to thought; in the pure presence that no knowledge can circumscribe. The unnamable is something like the inexpressible *real* of everything a truth authorizes to be said." *Infinite Thought*, 49. So Alain knows what the unnamable is, but she presumes he does not "feel" it.

P 61 Dear Diary, In case I needed to clarify, Žižek is the collection of afterthoughts, Badiou the tautology of conjunct tautologies. Poetry insults philosophy! This is merely the condition of this work passed down by the statements of Alain Badiou, and so I excuse myself.

P 65 You are the horizon, In *Theoretical Writings*, the chapter "The End of Romanticism", Alain details a lovely idea about how Cantor's discovery of multiple infinities changes the way we might conceive of infinity and its visual symbolic equivalent, the horizon. The poet here argues otherwise, reclaiming the romantic horizon in a new way, in a romantic way, for her own thought of the real projective plane and also towards her amour.

P 65 Do you believe in all who work?, Badiou defines poetry as "approaching the void", but certainly there exist an infinity of definitions about what poetry "is", all of them reasonable and relevant. And, importantly, possible.

P 70 Sartre, a riff on Sartre's notorious idiom: "Love is hate."

$$k_2 + \alpha_2$$

P 74 Love is thinking for 2 (+), This statement is ambiguous. Alain says Love is thinking for 2. Katy maintains that love is thinking for 2, plus something else.

P 74 Greatness in small things, as stated in the epigraph, "the sadness of the true seen from a distance changes into the joy of being when seen close up." *Infinite Thought*, 81.

P 74 Marxist society converge to thrive, Katy is introducing a point, that poetry is also conditioned by politics.

P 75 The real is what we need, An example of a "poem poem" as defined by Alain, "The poem marks the moment of the empty page in which the argument proceeds, proceeded, will proceed. This void, this empty page, is not 'all is thinkable'. It is, on the contrary, under a rigorously circumscribed poetic mark, the means of saying, in philosophy, that at least one truth, elsewhere, but real, exists."

P 76 The political view, Alain describes his politics in opposition to the politics of the state, which are defined as, roughly, "non-thought" – repetitive gestures which do not actually approach or address the situation. See *Metapolitics,* throughout and p 62 for discussion specific.

P 76 Never break a heart, "the Good is Good only to the extent that it does not aspire to render the world good. Its sole being lies in the situated advent of a singular truth." This is the Katy character's singular truth. *Ethics*, 51.

P 80 Nothing-everything, a riff on Alain's definition of the void: multiple of nothing.

P 84 Love of one for n+1, This would actually correspond to Alain's definition of the Humanity function, but we'll run with it here. Poetic license.

P 84 The universal 'we're on equal planes', For Alain's discussion on equality see *Metapolitics*, chapter 6, "Truths and Justice". It's not particularly pretty to point out "constant inequality". So, I won't.

P 84 Derivative hole, She's really digging at him here, in effect categorizing his definitions of poetry and art – the singular truths – as little more than a repetitive cycle which is itself formulaic.

P 84 Derrida collapsed the derivatives market, "philosophy [risks becoming] what in one way it mostly is, an infinite description of the multiplicity of language games." *Infinite Thought*, 35.

P 86 The moment is total in my typewriter, sweet cheeks, "The poem is a purity folded in upon itself. The poem awaits us without anxiety. It is a closed manifestation." *Theoretical Writings*, 240.

$$k_3 + \alpha_3$$

P 91 Infinity and the End of Romanticism, The chapter is actually titled "Philosophy and Mathematics: Infinity and the End of Romanticism", Theoretical Writings, 22-40. It's a fascinating read. Badiou describes the mathematical reorientation of infinity from a place solely understood "at the horizon" to be a commonplace occurrence, actually the MOST commonplace occurrence of which finitude is the exception. The inversion, essentially. It is Cantor's set theory, his discovery of multiple and unequal infinities that marks "the end of romanticism". Romantic being the Romantic Philosophy of the Romantic Period. Personally I think, well, the romantic is hardly a thing tied exclusively to infinity, but I won't harp, I'll call it poetic. But she is agreeing with said analysis, and adding, poetry too should be conditioned by math.

P 95-96 I'll let y'all duke this one out.

P 96 Gauss' projective plane, please see the note for page 31.

P 96 New God as you call it, honestly this is from a YouTube video I don't have time to go back and find right now.

P 96 Like you said, The fundamental tenet of *Being and Event* might be the distinction that inconsistent multiplicity (or infinity) is the norm, while finitude is the exception. Inconsistent multiplicity meaning "being", which applies to all matter, as nature does not exist.

P 99 Event without anxiety, "Philosophy is required to ensure that thought can receive and accept the drama of the event without anxiety. We do not fundamentally need a philosophy of the structure of things. We need a philosophy open to the irreducible singularity of what happens, a philosophy that can be fed and nourished by the surprise of the unexpected. Such a philosophy would then be the philosophy of the event. This too is required of philosophy by the world, by the world as it is." *Infinite Thought*, 41. Well said Alain, well said.

P 106 Rabat, Alain Badiou was born in Rabat.

P 106 Haven't accused you of being an Islamist yet, In Islamic thought, each moment is reborn infinitely, so Alain's understanding of infinite multiplicity as the fabric of Being, I think, approaches a convergence with some tenets of Islamic thought.

P 106 Truth is a hole, "The subject of a truth demands the indiscernible" *Infinite Thought*, 47.

P 106 Breathe the joy back into it, Poetry, as previously noted is looking at the small with *jouissance* (enjoyment).

P 108 The only thing that's formless is God, "There is no structure of being" *Being and Event*, 26. Essentially there could be two less compatible statements. But to the poet, who is obsessed with questions of form, the only thing that's formless, is God. But we circle back to her original point, which is that if the only thing that's formless is God, and if we are in the real projective plane, and infinity is right now...then Katy and Alain meet at the horizon.

$$k_n + \alpha_n$$

P 114 Leprechauns, This poem represents the image of a future between Katy and Alain, the Platonic image on the wall, if you will.

P 117 The way Heidegger had us, "Heidegger has subtracted the poem from philosophical knowledge, to render it truth." *Infinite Thought*, 73. "Heidegger...prophesizes a reactivation of the Sacred in an indecipherable coupling of the saying of the poets and the thinking of the thinkers." *Infinite Thought*, 74. Roughly, Heidegger determines that there is little at the end of deconstruction, except the poem.

P 119 We meet at infinity, Here, Katy's reasoning and Alain's reasoning converge: "The amorous procedure, which deploys the truth of difference or sexuation (rather than of the collective), proceeds from the 1 to the infinite through the mediation of the two." *Politics and Metaphysics*, 151.

$$k_{n+1} + \alpha_{n+1}$$

P 123 Einstein truth, Einstein famously had a contract with his wife that she only talk to him on certain days of the week so he could work.

P 124 Gil Scott-Heron, Lines from "Where Did the Night Go" from the 13th and final studio recording album "I'm New Here", XL Recordings, 2010.

P 126 I'll forgo all the details, "The philosophical place, the place of the occurrence, or the proving ground of the true, when seen from a distance, is, for most people, melancholic." *Infinite Thought*, 80.

P 128 If I don't believe in thought, "Philosophy only summons the poem for itself at the point at which this separation must expose what the argument, which frames and borders it, can only sustain by returning to what made it possible: the effective singularity of a truth procedure, singularity that is in the bathing pool, in the winding sheet, in the source of sense." Yes dear, that's pretty good. *Infinite Thought.*

P 131 'Like a stirring wheat field', "This 'all alone' of the poem... is a purity folded in upon itself. The poem awaits us without anxiety. It is a closed manifestation. It is like a fan that our simple gaze unfolds." *Theoretical Essays*, p 240.

P 132 If your mind leaves the axiom-checker on hold, "They [poetry] require the primordial defection of the donation of sense, absence, abnegation in regards to sense. Or rather, indecency. They require that truth procedures be subtracted from the eventual singularity that weaves them into the real, and that knots them to sense in the mode of traversing the latter, of hollowing it out. They thus require that truth procedures be disengaged from their [poetry's] subjective escort, including the pleasure of the object delivered there." *Infinite Thought*, 77.

$$k_{n+2} + \alpha_{n+2}$$

P 145 Endymion, John Keat's most famous long poem is called Endymion. It famously begins "A thing of beauty is a joy forever."

P 146 See T.S. Elliot, wrote perhaps two of the most wonderful poems in the English language, and the remainder of his output is shockingly spare and boring. Some connect this late career boringness with his ties to the CIA.

P 147 'Love what you will never believe twice', Alain, somewhere. What he liked to say at cocktail parties. jk. *Ethics*, 52.

P 149 This word finitude, Finitude as the exception to infinity.

P 152 is a conceptual poem taken from Alain's writing in *Metaphysics*, page 145. The original passage refers to political events (not poetic events) and the State (not the intellect). I replaced Alain's terms of politics (politics, political event, etc.) with poetry (poetry, poetic events, etc.) and the State with appropriate versions of "intellect".

P 154 Multiplicity inconsistent, "Why is the infinite multiplicity of the multiple like the image of a dream? Why this nocturne, this sleep of thought, to glimpse the dissemination of all supposed atoms? Simply because the inconsistent multiple is actually unthinkable as such. All thought supposes a situation of the thinkable, which is to say a structure, a count-as-one, in which the presented multiple is consistent and numerable. Consequently, the inconsistent multiple is solely – before the one-effect in which it is structured – an ungraspable horizon of being... There is no form of the object for thought which is capable of gathering together the pure multiple, the multiple-without-one, and making it consist: the pure multiple scarcely occurs in presentation before it has already dissipated; its non-occurrence is like the flight of scenes from a dream." *Being and Event*, 34.

P 155 "Pure Being = math", "Mathematics is rather the sole discourse which 'knows' absolutely what it is talking about: being, as such, despite the fact that there is no need for this knowledge to be reflected in an intra-mathematical sense, because being is not an object, and nor does it generate objects. Mathematics is the sole discourse, and this is well known, in which ones has a complete guarantee and a criterion of truth of what one says, to the point that the truth is unique inasmuch as it is the only one ever to have been encountered which is fully transmissible." *Being and Event*, 9.

P 155 Being-Qua-Being, "If one is concerned with being-qua-being, the multiple-without-one, it is true that non-being of the one is that particular truth whose entire effect resides in establishing the dream of a multiple disseminated without limits. It is this 'dream' which was given the fixity of thought in Cantor's creation." *Being and Event*, 36. I think here is Badiou's ultimate grace, where he admits the dream world, to let it stand on a mathematical justification (oh the social capital!).

$k_{n-1} + \alpha_{n-1}$

First, a note on the language of the chapter: "The powers of the language of the situation are themselves, to be sure, unrestricted: every element can be named from the perspective of a given interest, and judged in the communication between human animals. But since this language is in any case incoherent, and dedicated to pragmatic exchange, its totalizing vocation does not matter much." *Ethics*, 83. As the Event develops, blindly, the language sprawls, wildly.

P 162-165 Cultural Revolution, "Thus, a politics worthy of being interrogated by philosophy under the idea of justice is one whose unique general axiom is: people think, people are capable of truth....We encounter the same principle...during the Cultural Revolution in China." *Metapolitics*, 98. Though notably disapproving of the results of the Cultural Revolution, Alain is willing to admit it theoretically as an event whose underpinning concepts are valiant in their aims towards equality. Herein lies a totalizing disagreement for Katy. She considers, frankly, such a statement naming the unnamable: "Evil is the will to name *at any price*" *Infinite Thought*, 50.

P 163 It is not violence, "Mao's thesis concerning the immanent self-education of the revolutionary mass movement." *Metapolitics*, 99. Katy is arguing that whatever conceptual arguments Mao may have had, violence against the other *never* falls under the category of self-education.

P 165 Your humanity function is broken, "What is essential is that love is the guarantor of the universal." "What is Love?", 53. In short, she is claiming that Alain has lost sight of the pain (shattering of love) caused by the Cultural Revolution, and thus lost sight of his humanity.

P 173 Fine you wanna go there?, Here the argument descends into something evil. It is love, thinking as two, turning in on itself: "These are the figures of Evil, an Evil which becomes an *actual* possibility only thanks to the sole Good we recognize

– a truth-process." *Ethics*, 87. The truth process of thinking as two has become thinking *against* the two. "The ethics of truth is always more or less militant" *Ethics*, 75. Here, the militant battle for the bliss of the lovers splits on the battle of each for their own view.

P 173 Your thought Thermidored into, "Is thought obliged to endure Thermidorian frameworks of its own ruination?" *Metapolitics*, 139. In this case, if love is thinking as two, is love also obliged to undergo the thought process of its own ruination? And is this ruination as simple as a totalizing, negative critique of the lover?

P 175 Breaking bonds, "We have too often wished for justice to found the consistency of the social bond, whereas in reality it can only name the most extreme moments of inconsistency. For the effect of the axiom of equality is to undo the bonds, to desocialize thought, to affirm the rights of the infinite and the immortal against the calculation of interests." *Metapolitics*, 104. This is Alain's justification – breaking bonds – in support of his positive thesis on the Cultural Revolution. Katy obviously protests, on an even more fundamental level, against the wholesale idea that political emancipation necessitates the cold procedure of breaking bonds, and its necessarily corollary, love.

P 176 Death is merely a worldly principle of stability, Cute line, when taken literally. And here the poet departs, she departs into defending the set of all meanings of the line not included in the literal, for this is the difference between poets and philosophers: The poet cares for the entire set of meaning spilling out from a set of words. The philosopher cares for the specific meaning he has inscribed in words. It would be their endless misunderstanding. And by pointing this out she creates a final wound.

P 177 It's breaking my heart, Caught between two truths: the shared of the lovers' and self's singular. The breakup is the ultimate ethical moment, particularly what we say during those moments. Words are never more dangerous than in love.

$$k_{n-2} + \alpha_{n-2}$$

P 181 Nature does not exist, At the moment where love aught to be reconfirmed she parts from him, separated by doubt, unable to regain the common ground of a shared truth, lost. "Betrayal: to give up the truth in the name of one's own interest." *Ethics*, 91.

P 183 Democracy, "Love begins where politics ends." *Metapolitics*, 151. And where love ends, politics begins: "One shouldn't blame politics for what is, in actual fact, the result of a personal preference for the bound outpouring of the ego. By contrast, true instances of politics tend to manifest this faint coldness that involves precision." *Metapolitics*, 77. Shall it always be so? I think, there is an ethical point here.

$$k_n + \alpha_n$$

P 191 Wanted to be on the bottom, She refers to Alain's conditions, his schema in full. Where poetry resides, where philosophy resides – in short, how he sees the world. And she, well, she disagrees about her place. *Sous-entendus* of "gender" and fucking-forms not withstanding.

Back cover (This book should be banished), Žižek believes that all poets are fascists and should be banished as Plato decreed. No comment.

Malcolm X Park, Oh I LOVE that park!! Where the majority of *Dear Alain* was written. (& hell, he never claimed to be a zen buddhist.)

Epigraphs (in order of appearance)

Let us add ... Badiou, Alain. "What is Love?" One. Buffalo, NY: Umbra, 1996. P 37.

You dare to study philosophy baby ... Mayer, Bernadette. *Sonnets.* New York City: Tender Buttons Press, 1989. P 69.

Poem, Matheme, Politics and Love ... Badiou, Alain. *Infinite Thought.* London: Continuum, 1998. P 76.

It is fixed only by a nomination... Badiou, Alain. "What is Love?" *One.* Buffalo, NY: Umbra, 1996. P 45.

Love is nothing other than a trying sequence of investigations ... Badiou, Alain. "What is Love?" *One.* Buffalo, NY: Umbra, 1996. P 45.

Love is interminable fidelity ... Badiou, Alain. "What is Love?" *One.* Buffalo, NY: Umbra, 1996. P 45.

There is some sense in Plato's project ... Badiou, Alain. *Being and Event.* London: Continuum, 2005. P 54.

My soul cannot ...Jung, Carl. The Red Book. New York: W. W. Norton & Co., 2009. P 233.

The poem must be excused ... Badiou, Alain. *Infinite Thought.* London: Continuum, 1998. P 81.

Philosophers, says Rimbaud ... Badiou, Alain. *Theoretical Writings.* London: Continuum, 2006. P 247.

Little by little ... Badiou, Alain. *Infinite Thought.* London: Continuum, 1998. P 48.

The subject of a Truth... Badiou, Alain. *Infinite Thought.* London: Continuum, 1998. P 47.

The sadness of the true ... Badiou, Alain. *Infinite Thought.* London: Continuum, 1998. P 81.

Who is not familiar ... Badiou, Alain. "What is Love?" *One.* Buffalo, NY: Umbra, 1996. P 50.

Keep Going! ... Badiou, Alain. London: *Ethics.* London: Verso, 2001. P 91.

The point of the being ... Badiou, Alain. *Being and Event.* London: Continuum, 2005. P 35.

Is thought obliged ... Badiou, Alain. *Metapolitics.* London: Verso, 2005. P 139.

Evil is to want ... Badiou, Alain. *Ethics.* London: Verso, 2001. P 87.

So it is that the defeat ... Badiou, Alain. *Ethics.* London: Verso, 2001. P 80.

Ultimately true politics ... Badiou, Alain. *Metapolitics.* London: Verso, 2005. P 77.

There will always have been ... Badiou, Alain. *Infinite Thought.* London: Continuum, 1998. P 76.

An imperative function ... Badiou, Alain. "What is Love?" *One.* Buffalo, NY: Umbra, 1996. P 48.

The level of presentation ... Badiou, Alain. *Infinite Thought.* London: Continuum, 1998. P 127.

Author's Note:

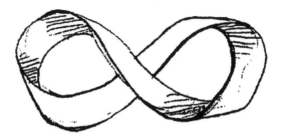

Can love, thinking as two, be enough to bond poetry which thinks as "elsewhere" and philosophy which thinks in distinctions? Despite the dramatic metaphor, in the end there is not a mathematic answer to such a question. Each answers their own way. Love the union of singulars.

Now then, is this poetry? If Badiou's conditions are all redoubled here, poetry on philosophy, philosophy on poetry, etc. then is it too much of a Gödel trick to ask? (The Indians wrote their calculus in verse, you know.)

Either transcendental way, and I don't really mind as long as it's transcendental, what I want to say is I think the relationship between philosophy and poetry is like what happens at the real projective plane: infinite, like a mobius strip. For when I think back on my own poetic departure, it happened when it happened, and why I'll never know (it wasn't really a choice), but it happened against all "reality" which had conditioned me in my life up until that point. And that was many things, including, fundamentally, definitions which all necessarily have philosophical under-pinnings, be they from texts or passed through the cultural conversation. That poetry, or writing, or art "reacts against" is true, but a reaction is also itself a relation. One cannot exist without the other. In this sense, I think, poetry is the fearlessness to depart, from the position of the self, in relation to all that is present in and up to that moment each poem is born – street wisdom or Alain

Badiou or whatever. Poetry is also Robespierre's eyes. Or the sun's, or the moon's.

Be it description or logic, this is how I saw it at that moment when the songs began (I also saw it as a sortof affliction, but that's a past sentence, pun intended, and isn't it odd how sometimes the things we hate at first we love later the most?) Perhaps it's a proof, perhaps it's my poetic "elsewhere". I don't really care to designate; it just is. To smile and laugh utterly naive to each moment's possible meanings whisping into the next moment's forgotten will always be more beautiful to me than the rigid lines of any conclusion. It's not that I (read we, if you prefer) can't, just that my preference is right now. As a way to perceive.

What I really want to say is that philosophy is not sovereign (thank you, Alain). And that poetry is is quite good at naming and defining itself! As it has been for thousands of years, regardless of whatever the philosophers have been saying. (What, what was that? Did you hear something?) And even, the practice of reading, interpreting, writing, and if you want to play that way... naming philosophy?

> "Something I always knew was it's all Aristotle's fault."
> – Bernadette Mayer

In some sense, poetry's and philosophy's irresistible urge to discuss each other for thousands of years is like the longest love affair in history since, well, Philosophy was born!

There is perhaps something in all of this of poetry's – and my – disdain for constraint or boundaries. Poetry, I think, is the undefined (and so, everything.) And as all writing is different from language in that it is about sex, I'll talk about Badiou's "woman": one who thinks love is what ultimately centers and binds the conditions of us all. If this is the meaning of "woman", then I proudly stand to militantly defend such a view with all my soul.

Love, always,
k

K. Bohinc was born November 19th, 1983 at 6:04 PM in Cleveland, OH. June 5th 2012 in the Western Roman calendar the planet Venus travelled directly between the sun and earth, an event referred to as the Transit of Venus. Occurring every 100 years or so in 8 year pairs, the Transit of Venus is of unknown and extreme astrological significance. In 2012, the Transit of Venus occurred at 15'44 degrees Gemini, in exact mathematical conjunction with the ascendant and north node of the natal chart of K. Bohinc.

For all who sheltered me while I dreamt.

THANK YOU PARENTS. THANK YOU BROTHER. THANK YOU POETS. THANK YOU LOVERS. THANK YOU FRIENDS. THANK YOU SHEENA GREWAL and JULIANA SPAHR for completion & CHRISTINA LIVA for beginnings. Thank you - forever - DC Poetry Community & MIDNIGHT IN DECEMBER – the collaboration led by Mel Nichols inspired by the 3:15 Experiment – where this work first formally began with SENOR PEANUT, ADAM MARSTON & LOVE. Thank you dearest publisher and dearer friend LEE ANN BROWN. Thank you conspirators MELISSA BUZZEO, BRANDON BROWN, ANDREW RUBIN & CASSANDRA GILLIG. And thank you, CAROLE GREENWOOD & STEPHEN ELLIS, for everything.

O! and to Cristobal Amunategui, Eduardo Cadava, Slavoj Žižek and Alain Badiou, luck and fearlessness, for your time, audience, grace and attention. Thank you!

GUESTCHECK™

Date	Table	Guests	Server	685097

APPT–SOUP/SAL–ENTREE–VEG/POT–DESSERT–BEV

Dear Alain

I always feel ~~somehow~~
a glow, the best, when
I confess + agreed
and they say no
and explain to me
why I'm wrong. There's
There's It's the last
thing. The integrality
of learning. It's not
commodified. No
power. No help or
hospitality. It's a
gift. Love y— | Tax | K.

Total

Thank You — Please Come Again